HMH Florida Science

FLORIDA STATEWIDE SCIENCE ASSESSMENT (FSSA) REVIEW AND PRACTICE

GRADE 5 STUDENT BOOKLET

Houghton Mifflin Harcourt™

To the Student..2

Diagnostic Tests

Science Benchmark Reviews

FSSA Practice Test

To the Student

Use the next two pages to find out about the types of questions that appear on the FSSA test given in Grade 5 and to see how your answers will be evaluated.

Multiple-Choice Questions

Most questions on the FSSA are multiple-choice. In these types of questions, four answer choices are given. The following tips will help you answer multiple-choice questions.

1. Read the question carefully. Restate the question in your own words.

2. Watch for key words such as **best, most, least, not,** or **except**.

3. Some questions may include tables, graphs, diagrams, or pictures. Be sure to study these carefully before choosing an answer.

4. Find the best answer for the question. Fill in the answer bubble for that answer. Do not make any stray marks around answer spaces.

1 Hawks are born with the ability to fly very fast so that they can catch their prey. This is called —

    A desire

    B hunger

    C swiftness

    D aerodynamics

Nature of Science

DIRECTIONS

Read each question carefully. Determine the best answer to the question from the answer choices provided. Then fill in the answer on your answer sheet.

1 In the forests of Sumatra where orangutans live, trees continue to be cut down for use as lumber. While studying habitat loss, students find this graph that shows what was happening to the population around the turn of the century.

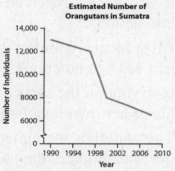

Estimated Number of Orangutans in Sumatra

Based on evidence in the graph, what was **most likely** the population of orangutans in 2014?

A 6,500

B 7,000

C 5,000

D 2,000

2 J.P. and Rosa investigate ways to grow tomatoes. They use three types of tomato plants and different amounts of fertilizer. They water each plant with 20 mL water every other day. They recorded the growth rate of each plant in the table below.

Growth	Big Boy	Roma	Beefsteak
Week 2	5 cm	3 cm	5 cm
Week 4	12 cm	5 cm	13 cm
Week 6	16 cm	9 cm	18 cm

J.P. and Rosa decide that the Big Boy and Beefsteak tomatoes grew best, but their results cannot be reproduced. Which mistake did they make?

F J. P. and Rosa would have had better results if they only used one type of tomato.

G Every plant is an individual, just like people. So, some grow faster than others.

H J. P. and Rosa needed to water their tomato plants every day to be more successful.

I J.P. and Rosa needed to use the same amounts of fertilizer for each type of tomato.

3 By 2050, a state plans to use only renewable resources (biofuel, wind, solar, and water) to generate electrical energy. This table shows resources the state used in 2015.

Energy Sources in 2015	Percentage Used
biofuel	14%
coal	17%
natural gas	32%
petroleum	25%
solar power	12%

Based on this evidence, which percentage of energy used in 2015 came from renewable resources?

A 26%

B 29%

C 43%

D 69%

4 Several students took part in a bird census for the month of October. Each student wrote a report to summarize their findings. Which has the **most** accurate empirical observation from their census?

F Jake: There were plenty of birds flying north on Saturday.

G Carla: I saw three types of birds I could not recognize.

H Jun: I counted 42 tree swallows and 112 purple martins in three hours.

I Esteban: Most of the birds I saw, like ducks and flamingos, live in Florida all year long.

5 Mr. Howell's fifth grade is making homemade lava lamps. Each student is given the same materials: one clean, clear 600 mL soda bottle with a plastic cap; two fizzy antacid tablets; food coloring; 100 mL of vegetable oil; and 500 mL of water. They follow a set of specific instructions and record their results in their science notebooks. What makes this a replicable, or repeatable, experiment?

A Every student received a set of instructions.

B All students recorded the steps in a science notebook.

C Everyone in the class is making his or her own lava lamp.

D The materials were measured out and added in the order listed in the instructions.

6 Which contains empirical evidence about the climate in Tallahassee?

F Tallahassee has hot, humid summers and cold, dry winters.

G Last January, Tallahassee experienced a week of freezing weather.

H In Tallahassee, there is less rain in January than in June or July.

I The average daily temperature in Tallahassee in January is 63.5 °F.

7 Tran is doing an investigation that involves heating water. He wants to see how long it takes for the water to boil. Is this the correct tool to use?

A Yes, it is a thermometer and measures heat.

B No, the thermometer only goes to 50 °C, which is not the boiling point of water.

C Yes, when the thermometer reads 0 °C, the water is boiling.

D No, this thermometer is for use in a refrigerator where meat is kept cold.

8 Jenna goes to the doctor who looks at her throat, swabs it, and sends the swab to a laboratory. The technician observes bacteria. The doctor gets the report and writes a prescription. Which produced empirical evidence?

F The doctor looks at her throat.

G Her doctor takes a swab and sends it to a laboratory.

H The laboratory technician observes bacteria on the slide.

I The doctor gets the report and writes a prescription.

9 As part of an experiment, Jenna measured the mass of the red cube.

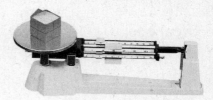

Which **best** describes why she should record her experimental procedure?

A The exact experiment can be repeated by others, and the results can be compared.

B The data will help others to find other properties of the red block.

C By writing down her procedure, she does not have to tell anyone about her experiment.

D Others can change the experiment to get different results.

Name _____ Date _____

PLEASE NOTE
• Use only a no. 2 pencil.
• Example: ◯●◯◯
• Erase changes COMPLETELY.

Nature of Science

Mark one answer for each question.

1 Ⓐ Ⓑ Ⓒ Ⓓ

2 Ⓕ Ⓖ Ⓗ Ⓘ

3 Ⓐ Ⓑ Ⓒ Ⓓ

4 Ⓕ Ⓖ Ⓗ Ⓘ

5 Ⓐ Ⓑ Ⓒ Ⓓ

6 Ⓕ Ⓖ Ⓗ Ⓘ

7 Ⓐ Ⓑ Ⓒ Ⓓ

8 Ⓕ Ⓖ Ⓗ Ⓘ

9 Ⓐ Ⓑ Ⓒ Ⓓ

Earth and Space Science

DIRECTIONS

Read each question carefully. Determine the best answer to the question from the answer choices provided. Then fill in the answer on your answer sheet.

1 How are the stars in our galaxy alike?

    A They are all the same size.

    B They all give off energy.

    C They all have the same brightness.

    D They are all an equal distance from Earth.

2 Which natural resource found in Florida is nonrenewable?

    F phosphate

    G solar energy

    H water

    I wind

3 Which describes **all** planets in the Solar System?

    A have rings

    B have moons

    C have solid surface

    D have orbits around the sun

4 Which environment usually has very dry weather?

    F desert

    G grassland

    H rainforest

    I wetland

5 Which can cause weathering but **not** erosion?

    A ice

    B plants

    C water

    D wind

6 Which **best** describes the relationship between rocks and minerals?

    F Minerals are the building blocks of rocks.

    G Minerals are formed from broken down rocks.

    H Minerals and rocks are two words for the same object.

    I Minerals are formed when rocks are melted and cooled.

7 Which natural resource found in Florida is renewable?

    A limestone

    B oil

    C silicon

    D water

8 This thermometer shows the outdoor temperature. Which type of precipitation is **most likely** to occur?

F   hail
G   rain
H   sleet
I   snow

9 Which describes what takes place during erosion?

A   ice cracks a rock
B   plants roots break a rock
C   water makes a pebble smooth
D   wind blows sand across the desert

10 The diagram shows Earth's orbit around the sun. How long does it take Earth to complete this motion?

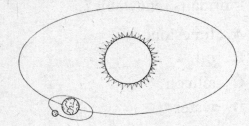

F   24 hours
G   1 week
H   1 month
I   1 year

11 Which is the **best** title for this list?

- Earth
- gas
- dust
- the sun
- objects that orbit the sun
- other stars and objects that orbit them

A   Objects in the Solar System
B   Things Found in All Galaxies
C   Parts of the Milky Way Galaxy
D   Things that Orbit Earth

12 Which part of the water cycle involves the change from water vapor to liquid water?

F   condensation
G   evaporation
H   precipitation
I   runoff

13 Which type of object found in our Solar System is shown in the diagram?

A   asteroid
B   comet
C   moon
D   sun

14 Hannah and Antonio observed the sun's position in the sky at different times of day. The table below shows their data. Which is the **best** explanation for their observations?

Time	Position of the Sun
8:00 A.M.	low in the sky, in the east
11:00 A.M.	high in the sky, almost overhead
3:00 P.M.	lower in the sky, slightly to the west
8:00 P.M.	low in the sky, to the west

F actual movement of the sun

G the rotation of Earth on its axis

H Earth revolving around the sun

I positions of Earth and its moon

15 Which label in the diagram identifies precipitation?

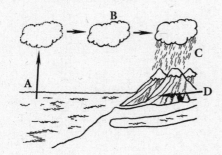

A A

B B

C C

D D

16 Franca and Jen observed the shapes of the pieces that formed when a mineral sample was broken apart. Which physical property of the mineral are they observing?

F cleavage

G hardness

H luster

I streak color

Name _____ Date _____

PLEASE NOTE
• Use only a no. 2 pencil.
• Example: ○ ● ○ ○
• Erase changes COMPLETELY.

Earth and Space Science
Mark one answer for each question.

1 Ⓐ Ⓑ Ⓒ Ⓓ

2 Ⓕ Ⓖ Ⓗ Ⓘ

3 Ⓐ Ⓑ Ⓒ Ⓓ

4 Ⓕ Ⓖ Ⓗ Ⓘ

5 Ⓐ Ⓑ Ⓒ Ⓓ

6 Ⓕ Ⓖ Ⓗ Ⓘ

7 Ⓐ Ⓑ Ⓒ Ⓓ

8 Ⓕ Ⓖ Ⓗ Ⓘ

9 Ⓐ Ⓑ Ⓒ Ⓓ

10 Ⓕ Ⓖ Ⓗ Ⓘ

11 Ⓐ Ⓑ Ⓒ Ⓓ

12 Ⓕ Ⓖ Ⓗ Ⓘ

13 Ⓐ Ⓑ Ⓒ Ⓓ

14 Ⓕ Ⓖ Ⓗ Ⓘ

15 Ⓐ Ⓑ Ⓒ Ⓓ

16 Ⓕ Ⓖ Ⓗ Ⓘ

Physical Science

DIRECTIONS

Read each question carefully. Determine the best answer to the question from the answer choices provided. Then fill in the answer on your answer sheet.

1 The state of matter with no definite shape or volume is a _____.

   A gas

   B liquid

   C property

   D state

2 Maya describes this unknown substance to Trevor.

Which words could she use to describe its texture?

   F cube

   G rough

   H shiny

   I soft

3 A beaker contains sand and iron filings. What is the **best** way to separate the sand from the iron filings?

   A Heat the mixture.

   B Remove them by size.

   C Shake the beaker.

   D Use a magnet.

4 Clem has a mixture of salt and water. Which process can he use to separate this mixture?

   F evaporation

   G filtration

   H magnetism

   I transpiration

5 Which is **not** an example of a chemical change?

   A burning

   B folding

   C rusting

   D wood burning

6 This water is boiling.

What **best** describes the change taking place?

   F change in shape

   G change in size

   H change in texture

   I change in state

7 One form of energy travels in waves and causes matter to vibrate. Which form is it?

A chemical

B electrical

C light

D sound

8 Air passes over the blades on this wind turbine and cause it to spin.

Which energy transformation has occurred?

F electrical energy to energy of motion

G energy of motion to potential energy

H energy of motion to electrical energy

I potential energy to electrical energy

9 Which statement about energy is **true**?

A Energy is a form of matter.

B Energy cannot travel through space.

C Energy has the ability to cause change in matter.

D Energy cannot change form.

10 The ball drops to the floor.

Which describes the relationship between potential energy and kinetic energy as the ball falls?

F The ball's potential energy increases, and its kinetic energy decreases.

G The ball's potential energy decreases, and its kinetic energy increases.

H The ball's kinetic energy decreases, and its potential energy increases.

I The ball's kinetic energy increase, and its potential energy increases.

11 Four light bulbs are wired on one circuit. Two bulbs are lit, and two bulbs are not. Which type of circuit is this?

A parallel circuit

B series circuit

C short circuit

D open circuit

12 This drill is plugged into an electrical outlet.

Which energy transformation occurs when Jamie pushes the button?

F electrical energy into light energy

G electrical energy into sound energy

H electrical energy into energy of motion and chemical energy

I electrical energy into energy of motion

13 A spacecraft travels in a straight line in space. The spacecraft moves at a constant speed, and no forces are acting on it. What will happen to the spacecraft's motion?

A The spacecraft will stop.

B The spacecraft will increase its velocity.

C The spacecraft will accelerate.

D The spacecraft's motion will not change.

14 Juan and Alex are pushing a box.

What keeps the box from moving even though Juan and Alex push against it?

F Juan and Alex are pushing with the same force in the same direction.

G The force of friction opposes the force applied by Juan and Alex.

H Juan and Alex are pushing with the same force in opposite directions.

I Juan and Alex are pushing with different forces in opposite directions.

15 What happens to the force of gravity between two objects when the mass of one object is increased?

A It decreases.

B It increases.

C It stays the same.

D It stops.

16 Charles pedals his bicycle with a force of 100 N toward the north. He travels at a constant speed.

Suppose the wind starts blowing with a force of 20 N toward the south. What will happen to Charles's velocity?

F His velocity will increase.

G His velocity will decrease.

H His velocity will remain constant.

I His velocity will not be affected.

Physical Science

PLEASE NOTE

- Use only a no. 2 pencil.
- Example: ○ ● ○ ○
- Erase changes COMPLETELY.

Physical Science
Mark one answer for each question.

1 Ⓐ Ⓑ Ⓒ Ⓓ

2 Ⓕ Ⓖ Ⓗ Ⓘ

3 Ⓐ Ⓑ Ⓒ Ⓓ

4 Ⓕ Ⓖ Ⓗ Ⓘ

5 Ⓐ Ⓑ Ⓒ Ⓓ

6 Ⓕ Ⓖ Ⓗ Ⓘ

7 Ⓐ Ⓑ Ⓒ Ⓓ

8 Ⓕ Ⓖ Ⓗ Ⓘ

9 Ⓐ Ⓑ Ⓒ Ⓓ

10 Ⓕ Ⓖ Ⓗ Ⓘ

11 Ⓐ Ⓑ Ⓒ Ⓓ

12 Ⓕ Ⓖ Ⓗ Ⓘ

13 Ⓐ Ⓑ Ⓒ Ⓓ

14 Ⓕ Ⓖ Ⓗ Ⓘ

15 Ⓐ Ⓑ Ⓒ Ⓓ

16 Ⓕ Ⓖ Ⓗ Ⓘ

Life Science

DIRECTIONS

Read each question carefully. Determine the best answer to the question from the answer choices provided. Then fill in the answer on your answer sheet.

1 Which organ does the **most** food processing to get nutrients and distribute them throughout the body?

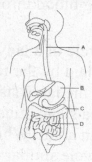

A A
B B
C C
D D

2 Which organism receives the direct flow of energy from the sun?

F cricket
G hawk
H robin
I weeds

3 How does this plant reproduce?

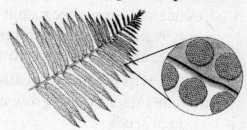

A cones
B fruit
C seeds
D spores

4 Which human organ system is **most** like tree bark?

F bones
G lungs
H muscles
I skin

5 Lucia plans to grow lettuce. She puts lettuce seedlings on a grid to hold them in place. Then she puts nutrient rich water in the pan under the seedlings. What will **most likely** happen?

A Lettuce will grow because it needs water, nutrients, carbon dioxide, and sunlight to grow.

B Lettuce will not grow because all plants need soil to grow and produce seeds.

C Lettuce will grow because it consists mostly of water, so it doesn't need soil.

D Lettuce will not grow because plants cannot grow unless they are planted outside in the sun.

6 How does this plant survive in the climate of a hot, dry desert climate?

F The cactus flowers at night so that bats can drink the nectar.

G The ribs of the cactus expand to store water in the trunk.

H The cactus grows very slowly, so it does not have difficulty in the heat.

I The spines on a cactus protect it from being eaten by animals.

7 Our kidneys are responsible for filtering blood. What other function do kidneys have in a human body?

A breaking down proteins

B controlling water and salt balance

C moderating body temperature

D moving blood through vessels

8 The life cycle of a ladybug begins with eggs laid by the female. The eggs enter the larva stage, followed by the pupa stage. Finally, the pupa becomes an adult. Which species has a lifecycle similar to a ladybug?

F alligator

G bat

H butterfly

I snake

9 What animal species would have the **most** difficulty surviving in this environment?

A ants, because they live in colonies underground

B owls, because they feed on mice, squirrels, and moles

C wolves, because they hunt in packs

D zebras, because they are herd animals that eat grass

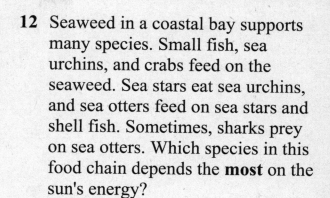

10 A shark can smell a single drop of blood in the ocean. The shark follows that scent hunting for food. Which animal structure is **most** like a shark's strong sense of smell?

F Echolocation helps bats fly find insects in the dark.

G A penguin finds its baby among thousands of other babies by its call.

H A great gray owl can hear a mouse running under 30 cm of snow.

I An elephant follows the trail of an ivory poacher by the smell of the stolen elephant tusks.

11 What physical adaptation helps this bird eat?

A a short, pointed beak for plucking seeds

B a sloped forehead that does not get tangled in shrubs

C light-colored feathers lying close to the head

D small eyes that do not get poked by thorns

12 Seaweed in a coastal bay supports many species. Small fish, sea urchins, and crabs feed on the seaweed. Sea stars eat sea urchins, and sea otters feed on sea stars and shell fish. Sometimes, sharks prey on sea otters. Which species in this food chain depends the **most** on the sun's energy?

F sea otter

G sea star

H sea urchin

I seaweed

13 Engineers built a dam to block the flow of water in a river valley. As a result, the environment changes from a river habitat to a lake habitat. Which river animals and plants may **not** survive this change?

A deer that use the river for drinking water

B willows that need a wet environment to survive

C fish that travel upstream to lay eggs and produce young

D dragonflies that lay their eggs on reeds in shallow pools

14 Which structure allows a tree to be a producer?

F branches

G leaves

H roots

I trunk

PLEASE NOTE

- Use only a no. 2 pencil.
- Example: ○ ● ○ ○
- Erase changes COMPLETELY.

Life Science

Mark one answer for each question.

1 Ⓐ Ⓑ Ⓒ Ⓓ

2 Ⓕ Ⓖ Ⓗ Ⓘ

3 Ⓐ Ⓑ Ⓒ Ⓓ

4 Ⓕ Ⓖ Ⓗ Ⓘ

5 Ⓐ Ⓑ Ⓒ Ⓓ

6 Ⓕ Ⓖ Ⓗ Ⓘ

7 Ⓐ Ⓑ Ⓒ Ⓓ

8 Ⓕ Ⓖ Ⓗ Ⓘ

9 Ⓐ Ⓑ Ⓒ Ⓓ

10 Ⓕ Ⓖ Ⓗ Ⓘ

11 Ⓐ Ⓑ Ⓒ Ⓓ

12 Ⓕ Ⓖ Ⓗ Ⓘ

13 Ⓐ Ⓑ Ⓒ Ⓓ

14 Ⓕ Ⓖ Ⓗ Ⓘ

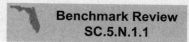

SC.5.N.1.1 Define a problem, use appropriate reference materials to support scientific understanding, plan and carry out scientific investigations of various types such as: systematic observations, experiments requiring the identification of variables, collecting and organizing data, interpreting data in charts, tables, and graphics, analyze information, make predictions, and defend conclusions.

The Practice of Science

All scientists try to explain how and why things in the natural world happen. Scientists answer questions that arise from observations of the natural world. A good scientific question is one that can be answered by investigation. An **investigation** is a procedure carried out to carefully observe, study, or test something in order to find out more about it. A scientific investigation always begins with a question.

Once a scientist has a testable question, it is time to plan an investigation. **Scientific methods** are ways that scientists perform investigations. The type of investigation can vary, depending on the question. All scientific methods use logic and reasoning.

Some investigations are experiments. An **experiment** is an investigation in which all of the conditions are controlled. Scientists study what happens to a group of samples that are all the same except for one difference. Not all questions can be investigated by experimentation. Scientists also use repeated observations to study processes in nature that they can observe but cannot control. Scientists use models when they cannot experiment on the real thing. Models can be used to represent real objects or processes. Scientists use models to study things that are too big, too expensive, or too uncontrollable to study in any other way.

Scientists use the results from their investigation to draw conclusions. The conclusion may answer the question or indicate that further investigation is needed.

Models

Some scientific questions involve objects that are too far away, too expensive, too big, or too complex to study by experimentation. Scientists can use models to address these questions. Scientists use models to draw conclusions and make predictions. **Predictions** are statements about future events based on information.

A variety of models can be used for different purposes. The best model is the one that most closely represents the real thing. The simplest model is a diagram or flow chart that shows relationships between objects or ideas. A physical model is a three-dimensional representation of the object or process. A computer simulation model is very useful for complex processes because it can change factors that cannot be controlled in the real world.

Experiments

Many scientific questions can be answered using experiments. An experiment is a procedure used to test a hypothesis. A hypothesis is a statement that can be tested and will explain what can happen in an investigation. An experiment should be designed with two or more situations that are compared. A variable is any condition in an experiment that can be changed. The idea is to keep all variables the same except one. This variable is the one you test. Among the setups should be one called the control. The **control** is the setup to which all the others are compared.

A **procedure** is the steps followed in an experiment. It is common for the procedure to be repeated multiple times. Repeated experiments increase the amount of data that can be considered. When the results are similar, you will have more evidence to support your conclusions.

All conclusions should be supported by evidence. The more evidence there is supporting it, the stronger the conclusion. Results are also used to evaluate the hypothesis. If the evidence does not support the hypothesis, the hypothesis may need to be revised. Further experiments can be designed to test the revised hypothesis.

Data Displays

Data displays summarize the results of an investigation. The type of display used depends on the type of data. The results of experiments are usually organized in a table. This makes it easier to compare setups. Sometimes additional calculations are required to make the results more useful.

Results are often displayed and communicated in graphs or diagrams. These types of displays summarize key points in the results. Data that show a change in time, or in another continuous variable, are often displayed as a line graph. Bar graphs are used to compare data from different categories. Circle graphs are useful when comparing parts to a whole. Non-numerical data can be represented in diagrams.

Science Tools

Some scientists investigate the natural world on location. Their investigations are often in the form of repeated observations. They use tools to increase the power of their senses. The tools they use depend on the question.

A field scientist might use a collecting net to catch small animals without harming them. The scientist can then take various types of measurements of various kinds. A hand lens can be used to magnify small objects to make observation easier. Cameras allow scientists to record events for later analysis. Photographs also help track and identify organisms. Scientists use computers to record and analyze data, construct models, and communicate with other scientists.

Some tools are too big or too delicate to be taken into most field locations. These tools are used in the laboratory. A light microscope magnifies things, or makes them look bigger. The object to be viewed is placed on a clear slide. The scanning electron microscope (SEM) can magnify an object up to one million times. The SEM shoots a beam of electrons at the object. An image of the surface of the object appears on a computer screen.

Measurements

Taking measurements is making observations involving numbers and units. Scientists around the world use the International System (SI), or metric system. The metric system is based on multiples of 10. In the metric system, base units are divided into smaller units using prefixes such as *milli-* and *centi-*. Base units are changed to bigger units using prefixes such as *kilo-*.

Length is the distance between two points. The base metric unit of length is the meter. Rulers, metersticks, and tape measures are tools used to measure length.

Time describes how long events take. The base unit of time is the second. Time is measured with clocks, stopwatches, timers, and calendars.

Temperature describes how hot or cold something is. Thermometers are used to measure temperature. Scientists measure temperature in degrees Celsius.

Mass is the amount of matter in an object. The base unit of mass is the gram. A balance is a tool used to measure mass. There are different types of balances; pan balance, triple-beam balance, and digital balance.

A spring scale is a tool used to measure force. Force is a push or pull. The base unit is called a newton.

Volume is the amount of space a solid, liquid, or gas takes up. There are two base metric units for measuring volume the cubic meter and the liter. A cubic meter is one meter long, one meter high, and one meter wide. A liter is the base unit often used for measuring liquids.

When a measurement is close to the true size, it is **accurate**. Accurate measurements are important when doing science investigations. Make sure a tool is not broken and that you know how to use it properly. Use the tool the same way every time. Measure to the smallest place value the tool allows. Be sure to use the correct units.

Student-Response Activity

❶ Which type of investigation–repeated observations, using models, or controlled experiments– would work best to answer each question?

• What type of shark visits a reef at different times of the year? _____

_____

• Does hot water or cold water dissolve sugar faster? _____

_____

• How does a rocket work? _____

_____

• How does the color of light affect plant growth? _____

_____

2 Karen hypothesizes that plants will grow better in water that has more minerals. She uses distilled water on tomato plants, tap water on bean plants, and mineral water on squash plants. What is wrong with her procedure?

_____

_____

_____

_____

_____

3 Identify which tools you would use to investigate each question.

meterstick   pan balance   magnifying lens   computer   net   camera

• How are two types of fish scales similar and different? _____

_____

• What do scientists already know about the surface of Mars? _____

_____

• Does the mass of a ball affect how high it bounces? _____

_____

• Which fish live in a pond? _____

_____

4 What conclusion can you draw from the graph?

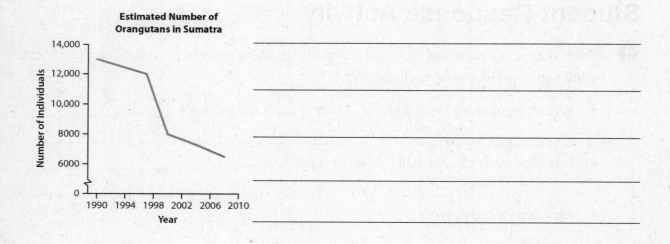

Name _____ Date _____

Benchmark Assessment SC.5.N.1.1

Fill in the letter of the best choice.

① Scientists want to determine if how loud music is played affects a person's blood pressure. Which variable should change in the experiment?

Ⓐ the type of music played

Ⓑ the amount of time the person hears the music

Ⓒ the volume of music played

Ⓓ the tools used to test the blood pressure

② Shayla observes the change from caterpillar to butterfly. She draws and labels each phase and shares her drawings with the class. Which statement **best** describes Shayla's investigation?

Ⓕ It involves modeling.

Ⓖ It involves experimentation.

Ⓗ It involves repeated observations.

Ⓘ It involves both experimentation and repeated observation.

③ Jermaine uses cell phone Internet service from provider A. Ricardo uses Internet service from provider B. How can Jermaine and Ricardo determine in a scientific way which Internet company has faster download speeds?

Ⓐ Read information from each Internet service provider.

Ⓑ Use a timer to find out how long it takes to download the same game.

Ⓒ Have each student download a different game and compare the time it took.

Ⓓ Ask ten friends who use each Internet service which one is faster.

④ Chen counts the number of people who visit the community pool each day for 1 week. He displays his data using a bar graph.

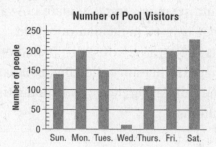

Number of Pool Visitors

How many more people did Chen observe at the pool on Friday than on Thursday?

Ⓕ 19

Ⓖ 200

Ⓗ 100

Ⓘ 90

⑤ Teresa has been growing plants without fertilizer. Now, she wants to see what happens to the plants when the amount of fertilizer is increased, as shown in the chart.

Plant	Amount of Fertilizer
1	No fertilizer
2	1 teaspoon every week
3	1 teaspoon twice per week
4	1 teaspoon once every two weeks

Which plant is the control?

Ⓐ 1

Ⓑ 2

Ⓒ 3

Ⓓ 4

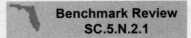
SC.5.N.2.1 Recognize and explain that science is grounded in empirical observations that are testable; explanation must always be linked with evidence.

Scientific Investigations

What All Scientists Do

Science is the study of the natural world. As a result, scientists try to explain how and why things happen in the natural world. Scientists use a variety of skills, including as observing, information collecting, comparing similarities and differences, and conducting investigations.

Observations and Investigations

A scientist's task begins with observing an unknown that needs more information to be explained. In order to answer this unknown, a scientist poses a question that can be answered through an investigation. An investigation is a procedure is carried out to carefully observe, study, or test something in order to find out more about it. A procedure is a set of steps a scientist follows during an investigation. The purpose of the investigation is to gather information, called **evidence**. Scientists think about what the evidence means, or what they can infer from the evidence.

Conclusions Based on Evidence

An **opinion** is a belief or judgment. It doesn't have to be proved or backed up with evidence. Opinions should not affect how scientists do investigations or how they draw conclusions.

A scientist should draw conclusions from the results of their investigations. Any conclusion must be backed up with evidence. It is important for there to be enough evidence to support a conclusion.

There are many ways to communicate, or share, the results of their investigations. It is important to communicate clearly so that others can repeat the investigation. Also, scientists can compare their results with those of others. They can expand on one another's ideas. In these ways, scientific knowledge can grow.

Student-Response Activity

❶ Define the following terms:

opinion _____

_____

investigation _____

_____

observation _____

_____

evidence _____

_____

conclusion _____

_____

❷ Describe how an incorrect conclusion might be drawn from incomplete or premature evidence.

_____

_____

_____

❸ A student makes a hypothesis that the water on the outside of the pan evaporates faster than on the inside. Describe an investigation the student could use to test this hypothesis.

_____

_____

_____

_____

_____

_____

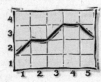

Benchmark Assessment SC.5.N.2.1

Fill in the letter of the best choice.

1 If an investigation was done using these birds, which is the **best** possible conclusion?

Ⓐ Since the bird on the top weighs more, it flies faster.

Ⓑ The bird on the bottom is more attractive.

Ⓒ The bird on the bottom flew from perch A to perch B faster over 10 trials, so it flies faster.

Ⓓ The bird on the top flew from perch A to perch B faster one time, so it flies faster.

2 Which is an opinion?

Ⓕ The boiling point of water is 100 °C.

Ⓖ Blue is the best color for parrot fish.

Ⓗ Bats use sonar to fly at night.

Ⓘ The ball rolled 10.2 feet over four tries.

3 For what can scientists use the data in the graph?

Ⓐ evidence

Ⓑ opinion

Ⓒ conclusion

Ⓓ investigation

4 What is **not** a possible observation of salmon swim upstream to spawn?

Ⓕ Salmon start their spawning season in the fall.

Ⓖ Bears easily prey on salmon as they swim upriver.

Ⓗ The average weight of a spawning salmon is 7.2 pounds.

Ⓘ Most of the salmon seem to be of adult size.

5 Why do scientists publish the results of their investigation in science journals?

Ⓐ They want to show other scientists what they are doing wrong.

Ⓑ It is a requirement for being a scientist.

Ⓒ The want others to support their opinions.

Ⓓ They communicate and share their findings so that scientific knowledge grows.

SC.5.N.2.2 Recognize and explain that when scientific investigations are carried out, the evidence produced by those investigations should be replicable by others.

Repeated Results

Scientific Investigations

Scientific investigations are procedures that are carried out to observe, study, and test something to find out more about it. An investigation's procedure are the steps followed by a scientist. During an investigation, a scientist observes an object or event under controlled conditions. The purpose of an investigation is to gather evidence that can be used support your conclusions.

Experiments

An **experiment** is an investigation in which all of the conditions are controlled. An experiment tests a hypothesis. A **hypothesis** is a statement that can be tested that says what the scientist thinks will happen in the experiment. An effective experiment will have two or more setups. One setup is the control to which all of the others will be compared. The difference in the setups introduces variables. **Variables** are conditions in an experiment that can be changed. In an experiment, you can only change the one variable that you are trying to test for each setup.

Recording and Analyzing Data

All observations should be recorded in an orderly way, such as in a table. Once the experiment is complete and all the data is recorded, it is time to analyze the results. Based on your analysis, you will draw conclusions. It is critical that all conclusions are supported by the **evidence**, or the information collected during a scientific investigation. Finally, based on your conclusions, you will decide whether or not the evidence supports your hypothesis. If not, you may have to revise your hypothesis, or even design a new experiment and continue to investigate. It's a good idea to repeat your procedure several times. Each time you will have more results to consider. If the results are very similar, you will have more evidence to support your conclusions.

Communicating your findings is important so others may learn from your investigation. To do this, your procedures must be clearly written down and your evidence neat and able to be reviewed. Your conclusions will be judged based on plentiful and complete evidence.

Student-Response Activity

❶ Define these terms involving scientific investigations.

investigation _____

_____

hypothesis _____

_____

control _____

_____

experiment _____

_____

variable _____

_____

evidence _____

_____

data _____

_____

conclusion _____

_____

❷ In an investigation, explain the best way to use variables in an experiment.

_____

_____

_____

❸ In science class, you are given four containers: one with pure water and three with different water solutions. You are asked to find which has the highest boiling point. Describe an experiment you can do to answer this question.

_____

_____

_____

_____

_____

Benchmark Assessment SC.5.N.2.2

Fill in the letter of the best choice.

❶ Why is it important to use accurate measuring devices when doing an experiment?

- Ⓐ to make sure substances are pure
- Ⓑ to ensure that the procedures can be repeated accurately
- Ⓒ to make it more convenient
- Ⓓ to avoid spilling the sample

❷ In an experiment to determine how far an object will slide on different surfaces, what is the variable?

- Ⓕ size of the object
- Ⓖ type of surface
- Ⓗ force that the object is pushed
- Ⓘ length of the surface

❸ What does this graph show?

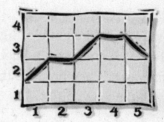

- Ⓐ data
- Ⓑ control
- Ⓒ conclusion
- Ⓓ hypothesis

❹ What is the **best** way to present data that is changing over time?

- Ⓕ circle graph
- Ⓖ table with time and recorded data
- Ⓗ line graph
- Ⓘ diagram of the lab setup

❺ What is **not** a reason to keep a neat lab notebook when conducting experiments?

- Ⓐ to be able to repeat all parts of the experiment
- Ⓑ to accurately record all data
- Ⓒ to record data analysis that supports conclusions
- Ⓓ to be able to accurately change data to support your hypothesis

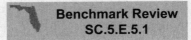
SC.5.E.5.1 Recognize that a galaxy consists of gas, dust, and many stars, including any objects orbiting the stars. Identify our home galaxy as the Milky Way.

Stars and Galaxies

Stars

Stars may look like point of light in the night sky, but stars are actually huge balls of hot, glowing gases. They produce their own heat and glow with their own light.

Stars form when gravity causes clouds of gas and dust in space to squeeze together. These particles are squeezed together under great pressure. Over time, energy stored in the particles is released as heat and light. A star is born. All stars give off heat and light, but they are not all the same. Some are cooler, and some burn hotter. They can have various colors.

Stars are classified by their color, size, temperature, and brightness. The color of a star can tell us about its temperature. The hottest stars burn blue, while cooler stars are red in color.

Stars have a wide range of sizes. White dwarf stars can be as small as a planet. Giant and supergiant stars are many times bigger than the average star. Larger stars tend to be brighter than smaller stars, because their larger size allows them to give off more light. A star's brightness is related to the amount of visible light it gives off.

Our own sun is a star. Even though it is a medium-sized yellow star, the sun appears much larger than other stars because it is so much closer to Earth.

Scientists use a Hertzprung-Russell diagram to show how stars vary in size, color, temperature, and brightness.

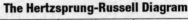

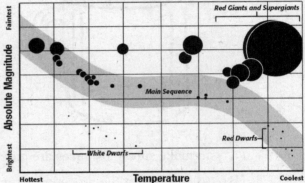

Galaxies

Stars are not distributed evenly in space. They are found together in groups of billions of stars, called **galaxies**, which are held together by gravity. Galaxies are made of stars, objects that orbit these stars, and clouds of gas and dust. There are billions of galaxies in the universe, with huge expanses of empty space in between them.

Our home galaxy is called the Milky Way, and it appears as a faint band of glowing clouds in the night sky. Galaxies are classified by their shape: spiral galaxies, barred spiral galaxies, elliptical galaxies, and irregular galaxies. Spiral galaxies have pinwheel-like groups of stars. Barred spiral galaxies have a center shaped like a long bar. Recent evidence suggests that the Milky Way is a barred spiral galaxy.

Student-Response Activity

1 How does the sun compare to other stars? Describe its similarities and differences.

_____

_____

_____

_____

_____

_____

2 What is the relationship of our own solar system to the Milky Way galaxy?

_____

_____

_____

_____

3 What does the Milky Way galaxy look like from Earth? Based on what you know about the Milky Way galaxy, why don't people on Earth see its spiral shape?

_____

_____

_____

_____

_____

4 Circle the objects in the list below that give off their own light.

Earth

moon

planets

stars

sun

Benchmark Assessment SC.5.E.5.1

Fill in the letter of the best choice.

1 Which describes our sun?

- (A) hot compared to other stars
- (B) very large compared to other stars
- (C) cool and small compared to other stars
- (D) medium-sized compared to most other stars

2 A star is blue in color. How does a star compare to the sun?

- (F) It is hotter than the sun.
- (G) It is cooler than the sun.
- (H) It is closer to Earth than the sun.
- (I) It looks brighter to Earth than the sun.

3 Which is **true** of the Milky Way?

- (A) The Milky Way galaxy cannot be seen from Earth.
- (B) The Milky Way galaxy is the only galaxy in space.
- (C) The Milky Way galaxy contains the planet Earth.
- (D) The Milky Way galaxy is very near to Earth's galaxy.

4 How are all galaxies alike?

- (F) All galaxies are the same size.
- (G) All galaxies are the same shape.
- (H) All galaxies are made up of many stars.
- (I) All galaxies are very close together in space.

5 Why does the sun look larger and brighter than other stars?

- (A) The sun is closer than other stars.
- (B) The sun is hotter than other stars.
- (C) The sun is larger than other stars.
- (D) The sun is cooler than other stars.

SC.5.E.5.3 Distinguish among the following objects of the Solar System — Sun, planets, moons, asteroids, comets — and identify Earth's position in it.

Our Solar System

The Planets

A solar system is made up of a star and the planets and other space objects that revolve around it. Our solar system consists of the sun, eight planets, many moons, many dwarf planets, an asteroid belt, comets, meteors, and other space objects. A **planet** is a large, round body that revolves around a star in its own orbit. The planets, in order from the sun, are Mercury, Venus, Earth, Mars, Jupiter, Saturn, Uranus, and Neptune.

The sun is the center of our solar system and is also the largest object in the solar system. The sun makes up more than 99% of the solar system's mass! All other objects that are in the solar system revolve around the sun.

Inner Planets vs. Outer Planets

Planets in our solar system can be classified based on distance from the sun. The inner planets are closest to the sun. The inner planets—Mercury, Venus, Earth, and Mars—are relatively small. They are very rocky and have thin atmospheres. The inner planets have large, solid cores at their centers. They have few or no moons.

The outer planets are farther from the sun. In general, the farther a planet is from the sun, the colder it is. The outer planets—Jupiter, Saturn, Uranus, and Neptune—are huge, mostly gaseous, and have rings. These planets are called gas giants, because they are composed mainly of hydrogen and helium. They do not have a solid surface, and their cores are very small. The outer planets also have many moons and ring systems.

Between Mars and Jupiter is the **asteroid belt**, a ring-shaped area where there are many asteroids. Asteroids are small bodies in space made of rock or metal. There are other areas of asteroids, too, but this is the main belt. Some of the particles are left over from the formation of the solar system. Other bodies have been added as they break off planets or enter our solar system.

The Solar System

Mercury Earth Jupiter Saturn Uranus Neptune

Venus Mars

Pluto was once considered to be the ninth planet in our solar system. Scientists decided to classify Pluto as a dwarf planet in 2006. A **dwarf planet** is a nearly round body whose orbit crosses the orbit of other bodies. Eris, Ceres, Haumea, and Makemake are four other dwarf planets in our solar system. These objects are very far away and hard to study.

The Inner Planets

Mercury, is the smallest planet in our solar system and is also the closest to the sun. It is less than half the size of Earth. Like the moon, Mercury has almost no atmosphere and a surface covered with craters and dust.

Venus is the brightest object in the night sky, after the moon. This planet is about the same size as Earth, and it is rocky. Its atmosphere is made up mostly of carbon dioxide. Venus can become very hot, reaching about 460°C (860°F). It is even hotter than Mercury because thick clouds surround its atmosphere keeping heat from escaping.

Earth, the third planet from the sun, is our home. It has an atmosphere made of mostly nitrogen, oxygen, and carbon dioxide About three-fourths of the surface of our planet is covered with oceans of liquid water. This makes Earth unique among the planets and gives our planet the nickname "the blue planet."

Mars is called "the red planet" because of its red, rocky surface. Its atmosphere is mostly carbon dioxide. Scientists have evidence that liquid water once existed on Mars. Mars has the largest volcano in the solar system, and it has dust storms that can last for months.

The Outer Planets

Jupiter is the largest planet in the solar system. It has rings and dozens of moons. There is a huge storm on Jupiter that has lasted for more than 400 years. The storm, like a hurricane, has a name—the Great Red Spot.

Saturn is best known for its rings, made of ice, dust, boulders, and frozen gas. The rings stretch about 136,200 km (84,650 mi) from the center of the planet! Like Jupiter, Saturn has dozens of moons.

Uranus also has many moons and rings. This planet rotates on an axis that is tilted much more than those of the other planets. Uranus looks like a top that has fallen over but is still spinning.

Neptune has many rings and moons and the fastest winds in the solar system. The winds can reach 2,000 km/hr (1,200 mi/hr)! These winds blow Neptune's Great Dark Spot around the planet. This spot is a storm about the size of Earth that is known to vanish and reform!

Moons

Some objects do not revolve directly around the sun. **Moons** are small natural objects that revolve around other objects. Many planets have moon. Earth only has one that revolves around it about every 27 days.

Comets

Comets also revolve around the sun. A **comet** is a chunk of frozen gases, rock, ice, and dust. Comets have long orbits around the sun. As comets pass close to the sun, part of their frozen surface begins to break away and turn into gases and dust. These particles reflect the sun's light and become visible as long tails. A comet's tails always point away from the sun.

Student-Response Activity

❶ Label this diagram of our solar system.

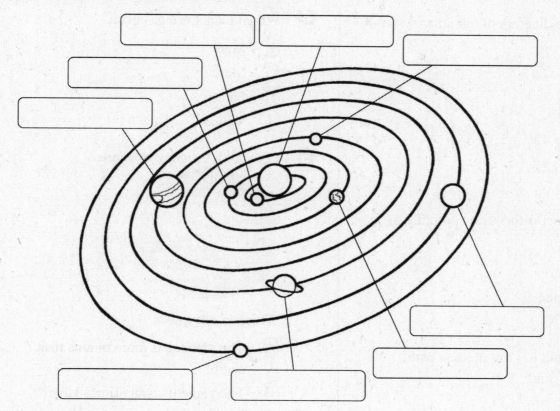

❷ How is the solar system diagram not to scale?

_____

_____

_____

_____

❸ What other objects are part of our solar system?

_____

_____

_____

Benchmark Assessment SC.5.E.5.3

Fill in the letter of the best choice.

1 Look at the diagram of our solar system.

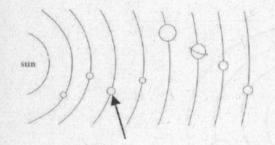

Which planet is the arrow pointing to?

- (A) Earth
- (B) Jupiter
- (C) Neptune
- (D) Saturn

2 Which planet has the shortest path around the sun?

- (F) Earth
- (G) Mercury
- (H) Neptune
- (I) Venus

3 Which planet has a rocky surface?

- (A) Jupiter
- (B) Mars
- (C) Neptune
- (D) Saturn

4 Which planet is a gas giant?

- (F) Mars
- (G) Mercury
- (H) Saturn
- (I) Venus

5 Look at this picture of Jupiter.

Which is **not** true?

- (A) The planet has more moons than Earth.
- (B) The planet is many times larger than Earth.
- (C) The planet's surface is much like Earth's surface.
- (D) The swirl you can see is a giant storm called the Great Red Spot.

6 Why is Pluto no longer considered to be a planet?

- (F) It does not orbit the sun.
- (G) It has too many moons.
- (H) It is not large enough to have cleared its orbit of debris.
- (I) It is too large to be classified with the inner and outer planets.

SC.4.E.5.4 Relate that the rotation of Earth (day and night) and apparent movements of the Sun, Moon, and stars are connected.

Movement of Earth in Space

Earth orbits, or travels in a path around, the sun. It takes Earth one year to complete one revolution around the sun. As Earth revolves around the sun, it also rotates, or spins, on its axis. Earth's **axis** is an imaginary pole going right through the center of Earth, from the North Pole to the South Pole.

Day and Night

People used to think that the sun traveled around Earth every day. That explained why the sun seemed to move across the sky. We now know that it is Earth's rotation that causes the sun to seem to move. The sun is not actually moving across the sky. If you stand in place and spin in a circle, you will see objects appear to move around you. The same thing happens each day with the sun and the stars in the sky.

Earth rotates once about every 24 hours. It is daytime for the half of Earth that faces the sun. It is nighttime for the other half of Earth, which is facing away from the sun. Earth is constantly spinning, so the parts of Earth experiencing day and night are constantly changing.

Earth Rotates on Its Axis

axis

The Moon's Patterns

When you look at the night sky and observe the moon, you may notice that it looks different at different times. Sometimes it is a bright circle, and sometimes you can see just a small sliver shining. The different shapes the moon appears to have are called moon phases.

new moon

waxing crescent

first-quarter moon

waxing gibbous

full moon

waning gibbous

third-quarter moon

waning crescent

new moon

Seasons

As Earth orbits the sun throughout the year, we experience changing seasons. Because Earth is tilted on its axis, different parts of the planet are closer to the sun at different times. When the part of the planet you live in is closer to the sun, you experience summer. When the part of the planet you live in is farther from the sun, you experience winter.

The Stars in the Sky

You can see many stars in the night sky. Have you ever noticed that the stars also seem to move? Some groups of stars seem to rise and set, like the moon and sun. Again, this is all because Earth rotates on its axis once each day. Like the sun, the stars appear to rise in the east and set in the west.

During the night, when the stars are visible, some groups of stars seem to move around in a circle that has the North Star, Polaris, in its center. Polaris doesn't seem to move much because it is located above the North Pole.

Just like the sun, the moon—whatever phase it is in seems to move upwards and downwards in the sky. The moon appears to rise and set in different parts of the sky and at different times. This is because the moon is revolving around, or orbiting, Earth as Earth spins.

Student-Response Activity

❶ How does the rotation of Earth on its axis affect the appearance of the daytime sky? How does the rotation of Earth on its axis affect the appearance of the nighttime sky?

_____

_____

_____

_____

_____

_____

2 How does Earth's revolving around the sun affect the temperatures?

_____

_____

_____

_____

_____

3 What are two ways that Earth moves in space? Which motion causes the pattern of day and night?

_____

_____

_____

_____

_____

4 How are the motions of Earth related to the length of one day and one year?

_____

_____

_____

_____

_____

Benchmark Assessment SC.4.E.5.4

Fill in the letter of the best choice.

1 Which causes the cycle of day and night?

(A) Earth's rotation on its axis

(B) Earth's revolution around the sun

(C) the moon's orbit around Earth

(D) the movement of the sun across the sky

2 What are two ways the moon's appearance changes over time?

(F) It changes speed and brightness in the sky.

(G) It changes orbit and brightness in the sky.

(H) It changes speed and position in the sky.

(I) It changes phase and position in the sky.

3 Why does Polaris appear to stay in about the same place at night, while other stars appear to move?

(A) Polaris is directly above the North Pole.

(B) Polaris is much closer to Earth than the other stars we can see.

(C) Other stars change positions in space, but Polaris does not.

(D) Polaris is much brighter than the other stars we can see.

4 It is noon where you are. Which statement describes the time of day on the opposite side of Earth?

(F) It is sunrise.

(G) It is sunset.

(H) It is day.

(I) It is night.

5 What observation supports the claim that Earth rotates?

(A) The sun appears to move in the sky.

(B) The moon moves around Earth.

(C) The moon seems to changes shape.

(D) The sun provides energy to Earth.

6 What causes the cycle of the seasons?

(F) the moon's orbit around Earth

(G) Earth's revolution around the sun

(H) the movement of the sun across the sky

(I) Earth's rotation on its axis

SC.4.E.6.2 Identify the physical properties of common earth-forming minerals, including hardness, color, luster, cleavage, and streak color, and recognize the role of minerals in the formation of rocks.

Minerals and Rocks

Minerals

Earth's crust is made up of rock, but not all rock is the same. A **rock** is a solid in nature that is made up of two or more minerals. A **mineral** is any nonliving solid that has a crystal form. All minerals form in nature. For example, granite contains the minerals quartz and feldspar. Metals such as gold and silver are also minerals. Different minerals have different physical properties. A physical property is a quality or characteristic that can be observed. Hardness, color, luster, cleavage, and streak color are some physical properties of minerals.

- **Hardness** is a mineral's ability to scratch another mineral. On the Mohs' scale, a mineral with a higher number can scratch a mineral with a lower number. The softest minerals score a 1.
- **Color** can be observed using the sense of sight. Different minerals have different colors.
- **Luster** is a mineral's ability to reflect light. Luster can be described using words such as metallic, earthy, and glassy.
- If a mineral breaks into pieces that have smooth, straight sides, the mineral has **cleavage**. Minerals that do not break along smooth lines have **fracture.**
- You can observe a mineral's **streak** if you rub it along a white tile. The color left behind is the streak.

The physical properties of the minerals that make up rock make different kinds of rocks useful for different tasks. For example, buildings and statues are often made of marble or granite. These rocks are hard enough to withstand weather.

Classifying Rock

Earth's rock is continually breaking down and reforming. On Earth's surface, weathering breaks down rock and erosion carries rock particles to new places. Beneath Earth's surface, heat and pressure cause changes in rock.

Scientists classify rock by how it forms. There are three main types of rock—igneous rock, sedimentary rock, and metamorphic rock. **Igneous rock** forms when melted rock, or magma, cools and solidifies deep inside Earth's surface. Igneous rock can also form on Earth's surface when a volcano erupts. On the surface, this melted rock, called lava, cools quickly and becomes solid again. This forms igneous rock.

Magma stored under Earth's surface can flow from a volcano during a volcanic eruption.

Wind and water break down rock on Earth's surface into smaller pieces, called sediment. As layers of sediment are deposited, the bottom layers press together by the weight of the layers above. Air and water in the spaces between the sediment are squeezed out. Over time, the sediments are cemented together and become **sedimentary rock.** Fossils are often found in sedimentary rock because of the way it is formed.

Deep inside Earth, heat and pressure can cause changes in the texture and mineral content of rock. When new rock forms this way, it is called metamorphic rock. These rocks have changed from one form to another.

For example, the metamorphic rock marble forms when high temperature and pressure act on the sedimentary rock limestone. The properties of marble are much different than those of limestone.

The Rock Cycle

After a rock is formed, it does not stay that way forever. The continuous process in which one type of rock changes into another type is called the **rock cycle**. For example, any rock can melt and become magma, then cool again, forming igneous rock. Any rock can be pushed below Earth's surface, where heat and pressure cause metamorphic rock to form. Any kind of rock can be worn away, become sediment, and form sedimentary rock.

Student-Response Activity

❶ Which types of rock can form above Earth's surface? Which kinds can form below Earth's surface? Give an explanation for your response.

_____

_____

_____

_____

_____

_____

_____

❷   Complete the chart with definitions of each physical property and how it can be observed.

Physical Property	Definition	How Can It Be Observed?
Hardness		
Cleavage		
Luster		
Streak		
Color		

Benchmark Assessment SC.4.E.6.2

Fill in the letter of the best choice.

1 On Earth's surface, rock breaks down into tiny pieces. The pieces settle in layers, become compacted, and stick together. Which kind of rock is formed?

(A) igneous

(B) metamorphic

(C) molten

(D) sedimentary

2 What causes rock to become metamorphic rock?

(F) heat and pressure

(G) weathering and erosion

(H) heating and cooling

(I) magma and lava

3 Which rock forms when magma cools?

(A) igneous

(B) metamorphic

(C) molten

(D) sedimentary

4 A mineral can be scratched by an iron nail. What can you conclude?

(F) The mineral's hardness is less than iron.

(G) The mineral's hardness is greater than iron.

(H) The mineral's luster is less than iron.

(I) The mineral's luster is greater than iron.

5 Josh rubs a mineral across a tile, and observes the color of the residue left behind. What property is Josh testing?

(A) cleavage

(B) sedimentary

(C) luster

(D) streak

SC.4.E.6.3 Recognize that humans need resources found on Earth and that these are either renewable or nonrenewable.

Natural Resources

You depend on natural resources every day. You breathe in air, you drink water, and you eat food that was grown in soil. The clothing you wear, your books, and your home are all made with natural resources. Even the resources we use to produce energy are natural resources. Life on Earth would not be possible without natural resources.

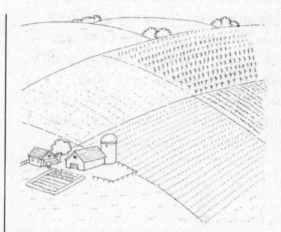

Renewable Resources

Some resources, such as water and air, can be used again and again. Other resources form quickly in nature and are easy to replace. Resources that can be replaced quickly are called **renewable resources**. A renewable resource is a resource that can be replaced within a human lifetime. These resources can be used again and again—if we use them wisely.

Air, water, plants, and animals are renewable resources. Water is essential for life. All the water we use is part of the water cycle. This cycle makes water usable again and again. Air is also reusable. Like water, it is a renewable resource. Like water in the water cycle, air is part of a cycle too. The carbon dioxide–oxygen cycle ensures we always have access to the oxygen we need from the air.

The food we eat comes from plants and animals grown on farms. Each year, farmers plant new crops in their fields so we don't run out of food. Crops such as corn and wheat must be planted each year. Many fruits grow on trees that bloom each year in orchards. New animals are born to replace ones that die or that are used for food.

Nonrenewable Resources

Unfortunately, many resources can be used only once. A nonrenewable resource is a resource that cannot be replaced in a human lifetime. For example, rich soils that are good for growing crops take thousands of years to form. If we remove soil from land or allow it to erode from farms, it cannot be easily replaced.

Some plants are essentially nonrenewable resources. Trees such as fruit trees do grow quickly and may be replaced in a few years. But an old-growth forest contains trees that are hundreds of years old. Once these trees are cut down, they will not be replaced for hundreds of years to come.

Fossil fuels, which include oil, coal, and natural gas, are nonrenewable energy resources. These are resources that cannot be made again in a reasonable amount of time and will someday be used up. Fossils fuels form over millions of years from the remains of dead plants buried beneath Earth's surface.

Minerals and metals are also nonrenewable. They occur in limited amounts in Earth's crust. Once these resources are used up, they cannot be replaced.

Florida's nonrenewable natural resources include phosphate, oil, limestone, and silica. Phosphates are minerals that can be mined, ground, and used in fertilizers. Petroleum oil is used as fuel and to produce many other materials, including plastics. Limestone is an important part of cement, and both limestone and silica are used in construction.

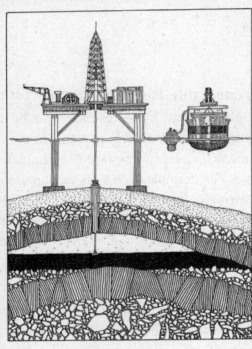

Many natural resources are used to produce energy. Like all resources, some energy sources are renewable and some are nonrenewable.

In many cases, using nonrenewable resources has negative effects on the environment. The burning of fossil fuels causes acid rain and has also been linked to global warming. People continue to use fossil fuels, though, because they are affordable and because the technologies to use them have been in use for many years.

As the world begins to run out of fossil fuels, though, their prices will get higher and higher. In time, people will not be able to afford them. However, people will still need a supply of energy to run their homes, businesses, schools, and automobiles.

Scientists and engineers are continually developing alternative energy sources that are renewable. Renewable energy sources can be used again and again. Examples of renewable resources include flowing water, wind, heat from deep within Earth, solar energy, and fuels made from plant and animal products. Wind turbines and solar panels are ways to use wind and the sun to produce electricity.

For example, the device shown below uses energy in the moving water of the tides as an alternative energy source. At high tide, a pool of water is filled. At low tide, the water is released from the pool through a turbine. The spinning turbine is used to generate electricity.

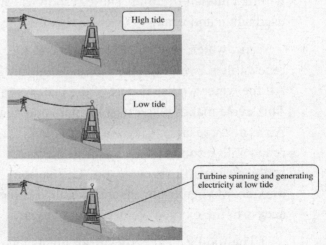

High tide

Low tide

Turbine spinning and generating electricity at low tide

Student-Response Activity

❶ Why are fossil fuels considered a nonrenewable resource, even though they are made from dead plant matter?

_____

_____

_____

_____

❷ Why is it important to find renewable energy sources?

_____

_____

_____

❸ Use the Venn diagram below to compare and contrast renewable and nonrenewable resources.

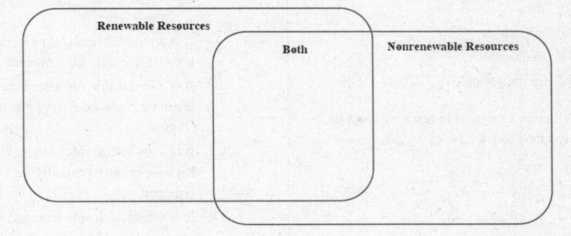

Renewable Resources   Both   Nonrenewable Resources

Benchmark Assessment SC.4.E.6.3

Fill in the letter of the best choice.

1 Which is a nonrenewable resource?

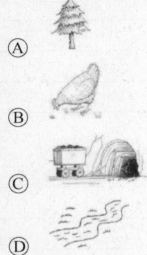

(A)

(B)

(C)

(D)

2 Which type of resources cannot be easily or quickly replaced once they are used?

(F) new

(G) reusable

(H) renewable

(I) nonrenewable

3 Which is a renewable resource used to produce electricity?

(A) coal

(B) wind

(C) gasoline

(D) natural gas

4 Why are minerals considered nonrenewable resources?

(F) They cannot be replaced.

(G) They can be replaced but not quickly.

(H) They cause pollution when used to make electricity.

(I) They take millions of years to form deep inside Earth.

5 Look at these objects. Which statement about them is correct?

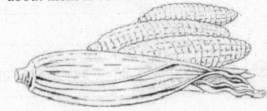

(A) It is a renewable resource because it can eventually be replaced.

(B) It is a renewable resource because it can be replaced within a human lifetime.

(C) It is a nonrenewable resource because it can eventually be replaced.

(D) It is a nonrenewable resource because it can be replaced within a human lifetime.

Name _____ Date _____

> **SC.4.E.6.4** Describe the basic differences between physical weathering (breaking down of rock by wind, water, ice, temperature change, and plants) and erosion (movement of rock by gravity, wind, water, and ice).

Weathering and Erosion

Weathering and erosion are two processes that cause changes to Earth's surface.

Weathering

Earth's surface is rocky and hard, but that doesn't mean it can't change shape. Rock can be broken into pieces, and those pieces can be broken into smaller pieces. The process of breaking rock into pieces is called **weathering**.

There are many causes of weathering. Gravity can cause rocks to fall down a cliff and break apart. Wind can also carry small bits of sand and rock. As the wind blows, these can act like sandpaper, scraping off more bits of rock from the rocky surface of Earth.

Water is a powerful agent that causes weathering. Moving water often carries bits of rock and sand, which can scrape along rock as water flows over it. Waves crashing on a shoreline exert force on the rock, breaking off pieces or rock from cliffs and rocks along the water's edge.

Water can also seep into cracks in rock. Since water expands as it freezes, if the temperature drops enough to freeze the water, the expanding ice will push the crack wider. Over time, chunks of rock will break into smaller and smaller pieces with repeated cycles of repeated freezing and thawing.

Living things can also cause weathering. Animals that scratch and burrow in the ground break large pieces of rock into smaller ones. Plants also cause weathering, as their roots grow into the ground. Tree roots can break up very large pieces of rock!

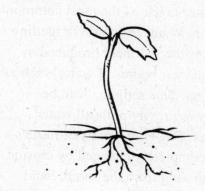

Erosion

What happens to weathered rock, once it has been broken up into small pieces? A great deal gets carried in a process called **erosion**. The erosion of rock can be caused by many different processes.

When wind blows over an area, it can pick up sediment—sand, soil, and small rocks. This sediment is carried along by the wind until the wind slows down. Then the sediment drops to the ground. This is how sand dunes are built up over time.

beaches can disappear in some areas and build up in others. Shallow rivers can become deeper and deeper over time, carving great canyons in Earth's crust.

Solid water—ice—also causes erosion. Glaciers are large sheets of ice that creep slowly over the land. They pick up rock and soil as they slowly move along. If they melt, they leave that rock and sediment in a new place.

Erosion can also happen because of gravity. For example, gravity might pull rocks down a hill. Sometimes small pebbles will roll, but gravity can make huge boulders fall, too.

Moving water is one of the most common causes of erosion. Water from rain or melting snow also washes the sediment produced by weathering into larger bodies of water, such as streams and rivers. This sediment can be carried far away as gravity pulls all water toward the ocean. Over time, parts of Earth's surface can be completely changed by erosion. Waves can wash sand from the shore. Sand

Student-Response Activity

❶ Give one example of wind erosion and one example of weathering caused by wind.

_____

_____

_____

_____

❷ Explain how gravity and water work together to move sediment.

_____

_____

_____

_____

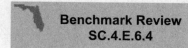
❸ Draw examples of how animals and plants can cause weathering.

Plants	Animals

❹ How does gravity cause changes to Earth's surface?

_____

_____

_____

_____

_____

Benchmark Assessment SC.4.E.6.4

Fill in the letter of the best choice.

1 Which process occurs when soil from a farmer's field blows away in a strong wind?

Ⓐ erosion

Ⓑ gravity

Ⓒ ice wedging

Ⓓ weathering

2 Which process occurs when a flowing river moves sand towards the sea?

Ⓕ erosion

Ⓖ gravity

Ⓗ ice wedging

Ⓘ weathering

3 What can result from tree roots growing into the ground?

Ⓐ erosion

Ⓑ gravity

Ⓒ ice wedging

Ⓓ weathering

4 Which is a cause of both weathering and erosion?

Ⓕ animals

Ⓖ sand

Ⓗ plants

Ⓘ water

5 How can a glacier cause erosion?

Ⓐ by washing sand from the shore

Ⓑ by picking up rock and soil as they slowly move along

Ⓒ by pulling rocks down a hill

Ⓓ by carving great canyons in Earth's crust

SC.5.E.7.1 Create a model to explain the parts of the water cycle. Water can be a gas, a liquid, or a solid and can go back and forth from one state to another.

The Water Cycle

Water on Earth

We can't live without water. Water covers more than three-fourths of Earth's surface. Approximately 97% of the water on Earth is salt water. We cannot use salt water to drink or water our crops. We would have to take the salt out of the water, and that is very expensive to do.

The other 3% of Earth's water is fresh. However, two-thirds of that water is frozen in the ice caps and glaciers. It is not available for our use. This means that only about 1% of all the water on Earth's surface is usable for humans and land animals. This fresh water is found in lakes, rivers, streams, and ponds, as well as in the ground and as humidity in the atmosphere. Water moves between Earth's surface and the atmosphere through a process called the **water cycle**.

Earth has what we call a closed system for water. We do not gain water from anywhere else, and we do not lose water to anywhere. The water you drink has been on Earth for billions of years.

Movement of Water

The water cycle is a continuous circulation of water and water vapor between Earth and the atmosphere. It is an ongoing process that has no beginning and no ending. The heat and energy for the cycle come from the sun. Water vapor rises from oceans, lakes, rivers, forests, fields, plants, and animals by the process of evaporation. The evaporated water is carried into the atmosphere, where it cools and develops

into clouds and fog through condensation. It falls back to Earth as precipitation, completing the cycle.

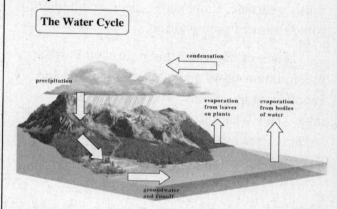

The Water Cycle

States of Water and the Water Cycle

Water exists as a solid, a liquid, and a gas at temperatures common on Earth's surface. Most of the water on the surface is liquid water. Water in the solid form is called ice. Water in the form of a gas is called water vapor.

Evaporation is the process in which liquid water changes into water vapor. The speed of evaporation depends on temperature. During the water cycle, the sun warms some of the water in the oceans, freshwater lakes, and rivers. The water on the surface evaporates. Plants absorb water from the soil and transfer the water through the stems to the leaves. Once the water reaches the leaves, some of it evaporates into the air as water vapor.

Condensation is the opposite of evaporation. In the atmosphere, water vapor cools to form tiny drops of water that we see as clouds. The water droplets form on tiny particles of dust, salt, and smoke in the air. As the droplets grow, they become heavier and start to fall. **Precipitation** is water in its liquid or solid form falling from the atmosphere to Earth's surface. Rain, snow, sleet, and hail are some forms of precipitation.

Much of the water that returns to Earth as precipitation flows across Earth's surface and is collected in streams, rivers, ponds, and lakes. This water is called **runoff**. Small streams flow into larger streams, then into rivers, and later into the ocean. Through

surface runoff, much of the water returns to the oceans, where a great deal of evaporation occurs.

Some precipitation seeps into the ground. Water that is underground is called groundwater. Groundwater trickles slowly down through the soil until it reaches rock. There, underground streams may form. Some groundwater returns to the surface as springs or in low spots on Earth's surface.

Student-Response Activity

❶ Label each image to identify each part of the water cycle.

_____ _____ _____

Name ______________________ Date __________

Benchmark Review
SC.5.E.7.1

❷ What role does the sun play in the water cycle?

____

____

____

____

____

❸ Describe how water changes state in the water cycle.

____

____

____

____

____

____

❹ Why is the water cycle important for living things on land?

____

____

____

____

____

____

____

Benchmark Assessment SC.5.E.7.1

Fill in the letter of the best choice.

❶ In which part of the water cycle does liquid water turn into water vapor?

Ⓐ circulation

Ⓑ condensation

Ⓒ evaporation

Ⓓ precipitation

❷ In which part of the water cycle does water return to Earth from the atmosphere?

Ⓕ circulation

Ⓖ condensation

Ⓗ evaporation

Ⓘ precipitation

❸ In which part of the water cycle do clouds form?

Ⓐ circulation

Ⓑ condensation

Ⓒ evaporation

Ⓓ precipitation

❹ Where does most of the water that evaporates on Earth come from?

Ⓕ creeks

Ⓖ lakes

Ⓗ oceans

Ⓘ ponds

❺ Which shows the source of energy for the water cycle?

Ⓐ

Ⓑ

Ⓒ

Ⓓ

SC.5.E.7.3 Recognize how air temperature, barometric pressure, humidity, wind speed and direction, and precipitation determine the weather in a particular place and time.

Weather and Climate

Look outside. It may be sunny or rainy. It might be stormy or windy. It might be hot or cold. **Weather** is the state of the atmosphere at a given time in a particular place. It can change from day to day or even hour to hour. Some things that make up weather are air temperature, barometric pressure, humidity, wind speed and direction, and precipitation. These elements may cause the changes we see in the weather. If you watch a weather report on television, you might see drawings that represent the weather that is predicted. These drawings represent some types of weather.

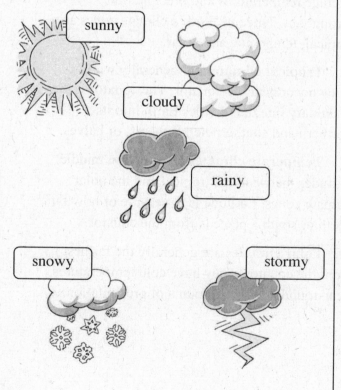

Measuring Weather

Scientists who measure weather conditions to study patterns in weather are called **meteorologists**. They use tools to measure air temperature, air pressure, humidity, wind speed and direction, and precipitation.

- Meteorologists use thermometers to measure air temperature. A thermometer is a tool that tells how warm something is.
- Air pressure is the weight of the atmosphere exerting force in all directions. A barometer is a tool that measures air pressure.
- Humidity is the amount of water vapor in the air. It is measured with a hygrometer.
- An anemometer measures wind speed.
- A wind vane measures wind direction.
- Precipitation is water that falls from clouds to Earth's surface. Precipitation can take the form of rain, snow, sleet, or hail. A rain gauge is used to measure the amount of rain that falls. Snowfall can be measured with a snow gauge or a ruler.

Temperature and Precipitation

Since temperature affects the state of water, air temperature affects the type of precipitation that falls. Air temperature changes with the seasons, with elevation, and with location.

- Rain is liquid precipitation that falls through warm or cool air. It occurs when droplets of liquid water that make up clouds become too heavy to stay in the air. Gravity pulls them down in the form of rain.

- Snow is solid precipitation that falls through cold air. It forms when water vapor in the atmosphere turns directly into solid snow crystals.
- Sleet is precipitation that freezes near the ground. It often begins as rain or snow. For example, sleet may form when snow partially melts as it falls through a warm layer of air and refreezes in cold air near the ground.
- Hail is solid precipitation made of layers of ice. It forms inside thunderclouds. First, wind carries raindrops high into the colder part of the cloud. The raindrops freeze and then fall through the lower, warmer part of the cloud, where another layer of moisture sticks to the hail particles. As the hail bounces around inside the cloud, layers are added and the hail becomes larger and larger before falling to the ground.

Climate versus Weather

Your area has certain weather patterns during the year. These patterns make up the climate where you live. **Climate** is the long-term weather patterns of a place. Climate is different from weather.

Factors that Affect Climate

Distance from the equator, elevation, proximity to bodies of water, and landforms affect the kind of climate of a location.

Most places that are close to the equator have warmer climates than places that are farther away. However, if a place has a high elevation, it will have a cool climate even if it is on the equator. That's why snowy mountaintops can be found in tropical places.

Oceans and large lakes affect climate, too. Because water heats up and cools down more slowly than land does, coastal places often are cooler in summer and warmer in winter than places far from the ocean.

Landforms, such as mountains, can affect the rain pattern of large areas. When wet air that formed over the ocean rises up the side of a mountain, clouds form and precipitation takes place on the ocean side of the mountain, giving it a wet climate. Then the dry air moves down the far side of the mountain, creating a dry climate, which is in a **rain shadow,** a place where it rarely rains.

Climate Zones

Places can be grouped into different climate zones. A climate zone is an area that has similar average temperatures and precipitation throughout. Three of Earth's climate zones are tropical, temperate, and polar.

Tropical climates are generally warm. They occur near the equator. The equator is the imaginary line that divides Earth into its northern and southern hemispheres, or halves.

Temperate climates are found in middle latitudes, between the tropical and the polar climate zones. Latitude is a measure of how far north or south a place is from the equator.

Polar climates are generally the farthest from the equator. They have cold temperatures year-round and low amounts of precipitation.

Student-Response Activity

1 Explain how the temperature of the air affects the type of precipitation that falls.

_____

_____

_____

_____

_____

2 What can a meteorologist learn from a barometer, and how can this information help forecast the weather?

_____

_____

_____

_____

_____

3 For each pair of locations, circle the one that is likely to have more snow.

    a. a high mountaintop   a town at the base of the mountain

    b. a coastal city in North America   an inland city in North America

    c. a forest near the equator   a forest far from the equator

4 Describe how lattitude, altitude, distance from bodies of water, and landforms affect climate.

_____

_____

_____

_____

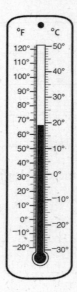
Benchmark Review
SC.5.E.7.3

Benchmark Assessment SC.5.E.7.3

Fill in the letter of the best choice.

1 Margie is moving from a coastal town to an inland city at the same latitude. What should she expect the winters to be like in her new city?

Ⓐ colder than the weather in her old location

Ⓑ warmer than the weather in her old location

Ⓒ rainier than the weather in her old location

Ⓓ about the same as the weather in her old location

2 Which tool do you use to measure humidity?

Ⓕ anemometer

Ⓖ barometer

Ⓗ hygrometer

Ⓘ thermometer

3 What does high air pressure usually indicate?

Ⓐ cloudy weather

Ⓑ humid weather

Ⓒ stormy weather

Ⓓ sunny weather

4 Look at the thermometer below.

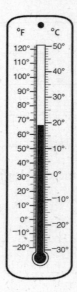

What type of precipitation is **most likely** at this temperature?

Ⓕ hail

Ⓖ rain

Ⓗ sleet

Ⓘ snow

5 Zack and Emily are hiking up a mountain. Which statement describes how the weather will **most likely** change as they climb?

Ⓐ It will become rainier.

Ⓑ It will become warmer.

Ⓒ It will become cooler.

Ⓓ It will become stormier.

SC.5.P.8.1 Compare and contrast the basic properties of solids, liquids, and gases, such as mass, volume, color, texture, and temperature.

Properties of Matter

What Is Matter?

Anything that has mass and takes up space is **matter**. All physical objects are made of matter. Mass is the amount of matter in something. **Volume** is the amount of space something takes up. If you could view an object through the most powerful microscope, you would see that matter is made of tiny particles called atoms. Each of these particles has mass even though they are so small you cannot see them. Different types of matter are made of different arrangements of atoms. Each type of matter has physical properties that you can see, smell, touch, taste, measure, and study.

States of Matter

Aluminum, water, and helium are all examples of matter that are very easy to tell apart. Each one exists in a different state. One is a solid, one is a liquid, and one is a gas. Do you know which is which?

Gold is a solid at room temperature. A solid is the state of matter that holds its own shape and has a fixed volume. A nugget of gold will neither change its shape nor change volume at room temperature.

Water is a liquid at room temperature. A liquid is the state of matter that has a fixed volume but not a definite shape. A liquid takes the shape of its container. You can pour liquid water from a pitcher into a glass.

At room temperature, helium is a gas. A gas is the state of matter that expands to fill its container. A gas does not have a definite shape or volume. Helium gas is used to fill balloons.

Other Physical Properties

You can use your senses to observe some of the properties of solids, liquids, and gases. You can use your sense of sight to observe the color, shape, and general size of an object. You can use your sense of touch to observe a material's texture. Your sense of smell tells you what a substance smells like, and your sense of taste tells you what it tastes like. Even your sense of hearing can help you observe the properties of objects. Can you tell the difference between a tennis ball, a pin, and a rock, just by hearing each one drop to the floor? Can you tell if a substance is a liquid or a solid using your hearing? Of course!

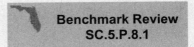

Using Tools

Other properties can be measured using tools. You can also observe whether a substance is attracted to a magnet. If you bring a magnet near various objects, you will observe that objects containing the metals iron, nickel, and cobalt will be drawing toward the magnet. Objects made of glass or wood will not be attracted to the magnet.

You can measure the temperature of a substance using a thermometer. Temperature is a measure of how warm a substance is. A substance with a higher temperature is warmer. You can also find out how much matter is in an object by measuring its mass, and you can measure how much space an object takes up by measuring its volume.

Student-Response Activity

Use the data table below to answer the questions.

Substance	Mass	Volume	Magnetic	Color	State at Room Temperature
A	27 g	10 cm^3	No	metallic, silver	solid
B	50 g	6.36 cm^3	Yes	metallic, gray	solid
C	40 g	40 mL	No	clear	liquid

❶ Which substance most likely contains iron? Use evidence to support your choice.

_____

_____

_____

❷ Which substance is most likely aluminum? Use evidence to support your choice.

_____

_____

_____

❸ Which substance is most likely water? Use evidence to support your choice.

_____

_____

_____

_____

Benchmark Assessment SC.5.P.8.1

Fill in the letter of the best choice.

1 Study this thermometer.

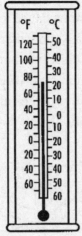

Which properties does water have at this temperature?

(A) It would fill its container.

(B) It would hold its own shape.

(C) It would not have a shape.

(D) It would take the shape of its container.

2 Which is a property of solids?

(F) takes the shape of its container

(G) keeps its shape

(H) fills its container

(I) can be poured

3 This chart shows the state of four substances.

Substance	State at Room Temperature
A	solid
B	gas
C	liquid
D	solid

Which substance is water?

(A) A

(B) B

(C) C

(D) D

4 Which characteristic of a liquid does the illustration show?

(F) It is wet.

(G) It has a fixed volume.

(H) It does not have a definite shape.

(I) It has a fixed volume and a fixed shape.

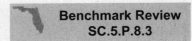
SC.5.P.8.3 Demonstrate and explain that mixtures of solids can be separated based on observable properties of their parts such as particle size, shape, color, and magnetic attraction.

Separating Mixtures

Mixtures and Solutions

A **mixture** is a combination of two or more substances that keep their identities. The parts of a mixture do not undergo a chemical change to form a new substance. Making a mixture is a physical change.

A fruit salad is an example of a mixture of different solids. The pieces of fruit are all mixed all together, but the apples are apples, the melon is melon, and the blueberries are blueberries. Each ingredient keeps its original properties.

And solids and gases? Mixtures can also be made up of solids and liquids, liquids and liquids, gases and liquids, or gases and gases. Air, for example, is a mixture of various gases. Granola with milk is a mixture of solids and a liquid.

Solutions

Sometimes one substance mixes evenly and completely, or dissolves, in another substance. A **solution** forms when one substance dissolves into another. A solution is a mixture that has the same composition throughout.

When you mix sugar or salt into water, you cannot see the sugar or salt grains anymore. Yet the parts of these mixtures still retain many of their original properties. Salt water and sugar water both look the same, but if you taste them, you can easily tell the difference.

Certain conditions cause a substance to dissolve more quickly in water. For example, salt and sugar will dissolve much more easily in warm water than in cold water. Crushing a substance into smaller pieces also causes it to dissolve more quickly, as does stirring the mixture.

Not all substances will dissolve in water. Sand does not dissolve in water, and neither does oil.

Separating Mixtures

Separating a mixture is not always easy, but since it is a physical change each part of a mixture keeps its individual properties. You can use these properties to separate them. For example, if you have a mixture of different beads, you can easily pick out the beads and sort them by color, size, or shape.

What other physical properties can be used to separate mixtures? Every substance has its own density. A less-dense substance will float on a more-dense substance. For example, some salad dressings separate naturally because oil floats on top of water or vinegar. Objects will float in water if they are less dense than water and will sink if they are more dense than water. A mixture of rocks and table tennis balls can be separated by adding water—the balls will float, but the rocks will not.

You can also sift mixtures to separate parts by their particle size. Sifting a mixture of rocks and sand through a screen will separate the two parts by allowing only the sand to pass through. You can also use a filter to separate some solids from a liquid they are in. For example, muddy water can be filtered to remove the soil particles.

You can use magnetism to separate a mixture if one of its parts is attracted to a magnet. For example, you can separate a mixture of sand and iron filings by passing a magnet close over the mixture. The iron filings will be attracted to the magnet, and the sand will be left behind.

Boiling is when a liquid rapidly changes to a gas at the boiling point of a liquid. Evaporation also changes a liquid to a gas, but it occurs at temperatures below the boiling point. During these processes, only the liquid particles leave the solution. The dissolved particles stay behind. For example if you allow sugar water to sit in a warm location, the water will evaporate into the air, leaving the sugar behind.

Student-Response Activity

❶ Explain how you would separate a mixture of salt and sand.

_____

_____

_____

_____

_____

_____

2 Explain how you would separate a mixture of soil, pebbles, and iron filings.

_____

_____

_____

_____

_____

_____

3 Sara wants to dissolve these sugar cubes in water.

List three ways she could speed up the process of dissolving the sugar cubes.

_____

_____

_____

_____

_____

_____

Benchmark Assessment SC.5.P.8.3

Fill in the letter of the best choice.

1 Which mixture would be **best** separated using a magnet?

Ⓐ iron filings and iron nails

Ⓑ iron nails and sawdust

Ⓒ sawdust and wood chips

Ⓓ salt and soil

2 Which mixture would be **best** separated using evaporation?

Ⓕ sawdust and wood chips

Ⓖ iron filings and iron nails

Ⓗ salt and soil

Ⓘ sugar and salt

3 Which mixture would be **best** separated using a filter?

Ⓐ sugar water

Ⓑ saltwater

Ⓒ soil in water

Ⓓ honey in water

4 Jed wants to dissolve oil in water. Which statement is **true**?

Ⓕ He should stir the water to help the oil dissolve.

Ⓖ He should raise the temperature of the water to help the oil dissolve.

Ⓗ The oil will not dissolve, because water must dissolve in oil.

Ⓘ The oil will not dissolve, because oil cannot dissolve in water.

5 Max has made a mixture of different sizes of rocks for a landscaping project. Data about the rocks are in the table below.

Rock Type	Diameter of Rock Particles (cm)
pea gravel	0.5
pond pebbles	1.0
river rock	2.5

Max decides that the river rocks are too large and wants to separate them out. Which is the best option?

Ⓐ Sift them out with a screen with 1-cm openings.

Ⓑ Sift them out with a screen with 2-cm openings.

Ⓒ Sift them out with a screen with 3-cm openings.

Ⓓ Sift them out with a screen with 4-cm openings.

SC.5.P.9.1 Investigate and describe that many physical and chemical changes are affected by temperature.

Changes in Matter

Matter can go through physical and chemical changes. Matter has physical properties that can be observed without change the type of matter. Matter can also change in ways that do not affect the type of matter. This type of change is called a **physical change**. When paper is cut, shredded, or torn, it is still paper. This is an example of a physical change.

Matter has other properties that cannot be observed without changing the identity of the matter. These properties are chemical properties. A **chemical change** results in a change in the identity of matter and results in the formation of a new substance. When paper is burned, it turns new forms of matter—hot gases and ash. This is an example of a chemical change.

Physical Changes

Changes in temperature can cause physical changes to take place. Did you know that each type of matter can exist as a solid, a liquid, or a gas? Some types of matter are solids at room temperature. Others are liquids or gases at room temperature. The temperature of matter determines its state. When enough heat is added or taken away, matter can change state.

For example, aluminum foil will change from its solid state to a liquid if its temperature reaches 660°C (1,220°F). It is still aluminum, but it is no longer a solid. This is a change in state. Changes in state are physical changes.

To form a seal between two metal pipes, a welder heats metal so it turns into a liquid that can be formed into a certain shape.

Water is a liquid at room temperature. If you put it in a freezer, its temperature decreases. At temperatures below 0°C (32°F), water freezes. Freezing is the change from a liquid to a solid. Solid water is called ice.

If you remove an ice cube from the freezer, it slowly warms. Eventually, the ice will begin to turn into liquid water. At temperatures above 0°C, ice melts. Melting is the change from a solid to a liquid.

Ice is solid water. It melts and becomes liquid water.

Place a pot of liquid water on a hot stove, and the water gets warmer. When it reaches 100°C (212°F), it boils. Boiling is the rapid change from a liquid to a gas. Sometimes, liquid near the surface will become a gas, even if the temperature is not at the boiling point. This is called evaporation, which occurs slowly and only at the surface of a liquid.

The boiling point of water is 100°C.

When a gas turns to a liquid, the process is called condensation. You have seen this process occur when water drops form on the outside of a cold glass. It might look like the glass is leaking, but that's not the case. Water in the form of a gas is called water vapor. It's in the air all around you, but you can't see it. The air's temperature is lowered by the cold glass. The decrease in temperature causes the water vapor to condense and form droplets of liquid water.

Condensation is the process of turning a gas into a liquid. We also call the physical drops of liquid that form *condensation*.

Chemical Changes

Changes in temperature can also cause chemical changes to take place. Many chemical changes happen when a substance's temperature rises. For example, when you place wood in a fire, the wood heats up and burns. The process of burning causes new substances to form, such as ash and smoke.

Cooking provides many examples of chemical changes that occur when the temperature of a substance increases. Frying an egg causes chemical changes that cause the transparent egg to turn white. Heating bread dough changes its texture and causes it to form a golden crust.

Student-Response Activity

❶ Describe how an increase in temperature can change each of the following materials. Classify each change as physical or chemical.

ice _____

_____

liquid water _____

_____

wood _____

_____

❷ Suppose an ice cube is taken out of the freezer. Predict how it will change over several hours.

_____

_____

_____

_____

_____

❸ Complete the cause-and-effect graphic organizer below.

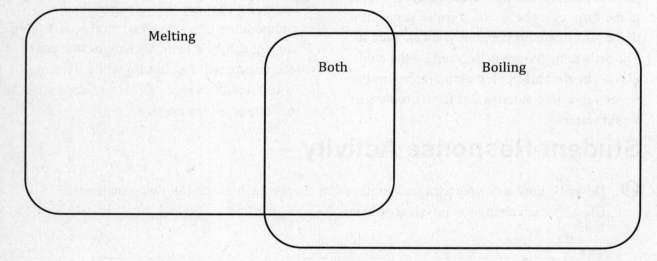

| Cause | | Effect
The liquid evaporates. |

❹ Complete the Venn diagram below to compare and contrast melting and boiling.

Melting   Both   Boiling

Benchmark Assessment SC.5.P.9.1

Fill in the letter of the best choice.

❶ Which process involves a decrease in temperature?

(A) evaporation

(B) boiling

(C) condensation

(D) melting

❷ Look at the drawing below.

Which prediction is **most likely**?

(F) The ice will melt, and condensation will form on outside of the glass.

(G) The ice will evaporate before it finishes melting.

(H) The ice will boil, and water will spill on the outside of the glass.

(I) The ice will condense and stick to the outside of the glass.

❸ Which is correct?

(A) Only water can change states.

(B) The solid form of water is called water vapor.

(C) At the right temperatures, any kind of matter can change states.

(D) A change of state is a chemical change because a new kind of matter is formed.

❹ You place a piece of bread in the toaster. A minute later, the toast pops up. What evidence tells you an increase in temperature caused a chemical change?

(F) The toast changed size.

(G) The toast changed shape.

(H) The toast changed state.

(I) The toast changed color.

SC.5.P.10.1 Investigate and describe some basic forms of energy, including light, heat, sound, electrical, chemical, and mechanical.

Forms of Energy

Energy is the ability to cause changes in matter. It is involved when matter moves or changes its shape. A change in temperature also involves energy. Energy can transform, or change, from one form to another. Energy is never used up. It just changes from one form to another. Energy can be classified into two groups—potential energy and kinetic energy.

Potential and Kinetic Energy

Potential energy is energy that an object has because of its position or condition. It is stored energy that can be used later. An object can have potential energy because of its position. For example, a ball at the top of a hill has gravitational potential energy because of its position and the force of gravity acting on it. Potential energy can also be stored in objects by stretching or compressing them. A stretched rubber band has potential energy, and a spring has potential energy when it is compressed or stretched.

Kinetic energy is the energy of motion. Any object that is in motion has kinetic energy. For example, if a ball begins to roll downhill due to gravity's pull, its potential energy will be changed to kinetic energy. Likewise, if the rubber band or spring is released its potential energy changes to the energy of motion.

Light

Light is a type of kinetic energy that we can see with our eyes. Light waves travel away from a source, such as the sun or a lamp, in a straight path in all directions. Light does not require matter to move from place to place; it can travel through empty space. This is how light from the sun travels through the vacuum of space to Earth. Light can also move through some matter, such as air or glass.

Light waves behave in different ways when they encounter materials. Some materials absorb the light, while others reflect it.

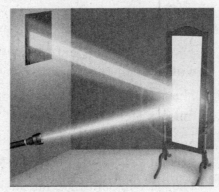

Light reflects easily off smooth, shiny surfaces such as a mirror.

Certain materials can also bend light. When light waves pass from one material to another, the light changes direction at the border between the materials.

Thermal Energy

Thermal energy is the total kinetic energy of the particles that make up a substance and is measured using a thermometer. Substances with a higher temperature are warmer. Heat is the flow of thermal energy from one object or substance to another.

What happens when you rub your hands together? They become warm—their temperature increases. Friction between surfaces produces heat.

Many objects that produce light also produce heat. Fire, for example, is hot and it gives off a great deal of light, too. Light bulbs, candles, and stove burners also give off both light and heat.

Sound

Sound is a form of energy we hear. Unlike light, it cannot travel through empty space; it requires a material such as air or water. Sound is produced when an object vibrates, or moves quickly back and forth. Each particle of the air nearby then begins to moves back and forth, bumping into other nearby air particles. This causes the sound to move as a wave. Sound energy moves, making it a type of kinetic energy.

Pitch is how high or low a sound is. A triangle makes a high-pitched sound, while a gong makes a low-pitched sound. When objects vibrate fast, they make a high-pitched sound. When objects vibrate slowly, they make a sound with a low pitch. Volume is how loud a sound is. Volume increases when more energy is used. Bang a drum softly for a soft sound and hard for a louder sound.

Electrical Energy

Electrical energy is the energy caused by the movement of electric charges. When you use electricity, you are using electrical energy. Protons and electrons have electrical charges. Protons have a positive electrical charge, and electrons have a negative charge.

Electrons are outside the nucleus of an atom. The electrons of some substances can flow. The flow of electrons along a path is called electrical current. You can use this electrical energy to make electrical devices work. When you plug them into a wall outlet, electrical current flowing through wires can flow into the device.

Mechanical Energy

Mechanical energy is the total energy of motion and position of an object. As a ball rolls down a hill, its potential energy decreases, and its kinetic energy increases. Its mechanical energy, though, stays the same.

Chemical Energy

There is also energy stored in substances, such as fuel, that is released when the substances are burned. This stored energy is called chemical energy. For example, wood contains **chemical energy.** When wood burns, it releases the energy as light and heat.

Batteries contain chemical energy.

Student-Response Activity

❶ Identify an example for each form of energy.

Form of Energy	Example
Light Energy	
Thermal Energy	
Sound Energy	
Chemical Energy	
Electrical Energy	

❷ How are potential energy, kinetic energy, and mechanical energy related?

_____

_____

_____

_____

❸ Can sound travel through empty space? Why or why not?

_____

_____

_____

_____

Benchmark Assessment SC.5.P.10.1

Fill in the letter of the best choice.

❶ What form of energy is in a battery?

(A) light energy

(B) kinetic energy

(C) chemical energy

(D) electrical energy

❷ Which has the least amount of potential energy?

(F) a ball at the top of a hill

(G) a roller coaster going down a hill

(H) a child at the top of a slide

(I) a car parked in a parking lot

❸ Which are forms of kinetic energy?

(A) light, sound, chemical

(B) electrical, chemical, sound

(C) sound, potential, thermal

(D) light, thermal, sound

❹ What form of energy can be absorbed, reflected or bent by different materials?

(F) sound

(G) electrical

(H) light

(I) mechanical

❺ What forms of energy does this object give off?

(A) light energy and thermal energy

(B) light energy and sound energy

(C) light energy and electrical energy

(D) light energy and chemical energy

SC.5.P.10.2 Investigate and explain that energy has the ability to cause motion or create change.

Energy Can Cause Change

Motion

Where are you located right now? Are you at your desk? Under a light? To the right of a door, or 2 meters (6 feet) away from the board? These types of words describe your position. Position is the location of an object. Every object has a position. The position of your nose is the center of your face.

When an object's position changes, the object is in motion. Motion is a change of position of an object. There are many types of motion. You can walk forward or backward. An elevator goes up and down. A pendulum swings from side to side. Things may move quickly or slowly. They may follow a straight, curved, or circular path. All types of motion involve a change in position.

Speed

How fast can you run? If you run faster than your friend, your speed is greater. Speed measures the change in the position of an object changes over a certain amount of time.

You can use words such as *fast* and *slow* to describe speed. Fast-moving objects change their position quickly. Slow-moving objects change their position slowly. You can be more precise if you use numbers such as 20 kilometers per hour or 5 meters per second.

To find an object's speed, you need to measure two things—distance and time. Distance is how far an object traveled. You also need to measure how long it takes the object to move that distance.

A cheetah is the fastest land animal. It can reach speeds of 112 km/hr (70 mi/hr)!

Energy and Motion

Energy is the ability to cause changes to matter. A force—a push or a pull—can cause an object to move. In other words, a push or a pull to cause an object change position—to be in motion. A push or a pull transfers energy from one object to another, which causes the object to move. For example, if you swing a golf club and hit a golf ball off the tee, the energy of the moving club is transferred to the ball, and so the ball begins to move.

When ocean waves crash onto the beach, energy of flowing water can flatten a sandcastle. The energy of moving air—wind—can move a sailboat across the surface of a lake.

An object's speed is also related to energy. When an object is in motion, it has kinetic energy. An object moving at a faster speed has more energy than it has at a slower speed. So a running cheetah has more kinetic energy than a walking cheetah.

Light

Energy does not always need matter to cause change. Light energy is a form of energy that can travel from one place to another without matter. It travels from the sun through areas of space where there is no matter. Some of this light reaches Earth. There, the light causes objects to be visible. Light from the sun also causes objects to warm up.

Student-Response Activity

❶ Which statements about energy are true? Circle all correct statements.

a. Energy is the ability to cause changes to matter.

b. Energy can only be transferred when one object pushes or pulls on another.

c. Energy can be transferred from objects that touch as well as through empty space.

d. An object moving at high speed has more energy than the same object moving slowly.

e. An object moving at high speed has the same amount of energy than the same object moving slowly.

❷ Explain how energy from the sun can cause ice cream to change.

_____

_____

_____

❸ How can energy of moving water and moving wind cause changes? Give an example of each.

_____

_____

_____

_____

❹ Describe two ways you could use energy to cause a wagon to move.

_____

_____

_____

_____

Benchmark Assessment SC.5.P.10.2

Fill in the letter of the best choice.

1 Which is **not** an example of energy causing motion?

- Ⓐ picking up a box
- Ⓑ holding a box
- Ⓒ placing a box on a shelf
- Ⓓ placing a box on the floor

2 Which describes a change caused by the sun's energy?

- Ⓕ A marshmallow toasts over a fire.
- Ⓖ Water for tea is boiled on a stove.
- Ⓗ Water in a rain puddle evaporates.
- Ⓘ A light bulb glows when the switch is turned.

3 Which description applies to the picture below?

- Ⓐ Energy from the paddle and the moving water moves the canoe.
- Ⓑ Energy from the paddle and the wind moves the canoe.
- Ⓒ Energy from the wind and the moving water moves the canoe.
- Ⓓ Energy from the wind and gravity moves the canoe.

4 Zelie used an electric fan to power four identical toy sailboats across a bowl of water. The data table shows how the distance and time for each sailboat.

Boat	Time (seconds)	Distance (inches)
F	42	24
G	34	24
H	27	24
I	31	24

Which boat traveled with the **most** kinetic energy?

- Ⓕ F
- Ⓖ G
- Ⓗ H
- Ⓘ I

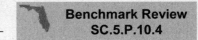
SC.5.P.10.4 Investigate and explain that electrical energy can be transformed into heat, light, and sound energy, as well as the energy of motion.

Heat and Electricity

Heat is the flow of thermal energy from one object to another. Heat always flows from a warmer object to a cooler object, which causes the objects to change temperature.

Conduction

Conduction is the movement of thermal energy between particles of matter that collide, or crash together. Conduction transfers heat through solids or from a liquid or gas to a solid. In order for heat to be conducted from one object to another, the two objects must touch. Particles of one object can collide with particles of another object only when the two objects are touching.

Convection

Heat can also move by convection. **Convection** is the transfer of heat through a moving liquid or gas. Think again about water heated in a pot on a stove. The water gets heated where it touches the metal pot by conduction. The heated water particles move faster and then spread farther apart. As a result, the heated water becomes less dense and rises. Cooler water sinks beneath it. This flow causes currents of warmer rising water and cooler sinking water to transfer heat throughout all of the water.

Radiation

Light travels from the sun to Earth's surface through space. These waves cause objects they strike to warm up. Heat transfer by conduction or convection needs particles of matter to carry energy. However, heat transfer by radiation can occur in empty space where there is no matter.

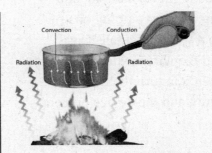

Conductors and Insulators

Materials that allow heat to flow easily through them are called **conductors**. Metals such as aluminum and copper conduct heat well. An **insulator** is a material that heat does not move through easily. Materials such as glass, wood, and plastic are good insulators.

Electricity

Static electricity and current electricity are two types of electricity. Static electricity is what causes socks from the dryer to stick together. Clothes in the dryer gain and lose electrons by rubbing against other fabrics. Some of the clothes obtain a negative charge by gaining electrons, and other clothes obtain a positive charge by losing electrons. Objects with opposite electrical charges attract each other, so some clothes stick together. Clothes with the same charge will repel each other, even if they are not touching.

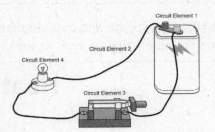
Using Electricity

Electrical devices, such as computers, toasters, and lamps, are useful because they transform electrical energy into other forms of energy, such as sound, light, thermal, and mechanical energy. When you plug one of these devices into a wall outlet, electrical current flows from the wires inside the outlet to the device. When you turn the device on, you close the circuit, and the device powers on.

Electrical Circuits

An **electric circuit** is a path along which electric charges can flow. For electricity to flow, the circuit must form a complete, unbroken, loop. A circuit with no breaks in it is called a closed circuit. If the path is broken, charges cannot flow. A circuit with a break in the path is called an open circuit. A switch on a circuit controls the flow of electrical current by opening and closing the circuit.

Electricity flows through the closed circuit. When the circuit is closed, the light bulb will light up.

In general, materials that conduct heat also conduct electricity. Copper wire, a metal that conducts heat well, is commonly used in electrical circuits. Plastic, an insulator, is used to enclose the wires to contain the electrical current in the circuit.

Student-Response Activity

❶ Classify these materials as *conductors* or *insulators*.

| glass | plastic | copper | gold | aluminum |
| silver | iron | wood | rubber | steel |

Conductors	Insulators

❷   Describe the energy transformation performed by each device.

toaster _____

_____

_____

_____

light bulb _____

_____

_____

_____

electric guitar _____

_____

_____

_____

television _____

_____

_____

_____

_____

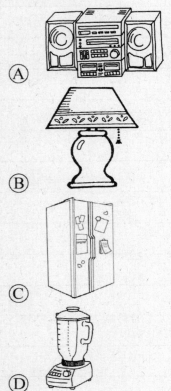
Benchmark Assessment SC.5.P.10.4

Fill in the letter of the best choice.

❶ Which shows a device designed to transform electrical energy into mechanical energy?

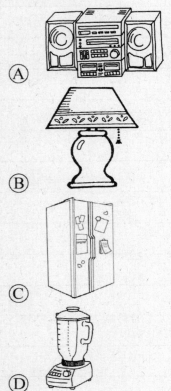

(A)

(B)

(C)

(D)

❷ What energy transformation takes place inside a toaster?

(F) electrical to light energy

(G) electrical to sound energy

(H) electrical to light and thermal energy

(I) electrical to sound and thermal energy

❸ Sandy built a circuit that would light a light bulb. When she connected the wire to the battery, however, the light bulb did not light. What is the most likely reason the light bulb would not light?

(A) The circuit was not continuous.

(B) The wire was made of copper.

(C) The switch was closed.

(D) The battery was not powerful enough.

❹ What energy transformation takes place inside a oven?

(F) electrical to light energy

(G) electrical to sound energy

(H) electrical to light and thermal energy

(I) electrical to sound and thermal energy

❺ Which is a conductor?

(A) glass

(B) plastic

(C) silver

(D) wood

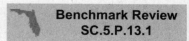
SC.5.P.13.1 Identify familiar forces that cause objects to move, such as pushes or pulls, including gravity acting on falling objects.

Forces

Pushes and Pulls

Push a door, and it moves. Pull the door, and it moves the other way. Pushes and pulls of all kinds are called forces. Forces are measured in newtons (N). The larger the force, the greater the change it can cause to the motion of the object. Smaller forces cause smaller changes. Sometimes more than one force can act together in a way that does not cause a change in motion.

Forces can cause changes in the speed and direction of motion of an object. Forces can cause objects to move, and they can cause objects to slow down and stop moving. They cause changes in the speed and direction of motion. If a soccer ball is still, it stays still until a force moves it. If you kick a soccer ball, it keeps moving in the same direction until another force changes its motion. The direction in which an object moves depends on the direction of the force that is applied to the object. If there is more than one force, the forces work together.

Balanced and Unbalanced Forces

Forces do not always cause motion. When two forces have the same size but work in opposite directions, they cancel each other out. These are called **balanced forces**. For example, if you and a friend push with the same amount of force on a desk but push in opposite directions, the desk will not move. However, if one of you decides to push with more force, however, the forces become unbalanced and the desk will move.

Friction

Friction is a force that opposes motion. It slows down objects that are moving, eventually causing them to stop. Friction occurs when two surfaces touch or rub against each other. For example, if you roll a ball across the floor, friction between the ball and the floor slows the motion of the ball. The friction acts in the opposite direction of the motion of the ball. Rough surfaces create more friction than smooth ones. So it is more difficult to push a box across a carpeted floor than a smooth wood floor because more friction is resisting the box's motion.

Gravity

When you push or pull on an object, you usually touch the object to exert a force on it. Friction is also a force that requires two surfaces to touch. But not all forces require contact. **Gravity** is a force of attraction between two objects. Gravity pulls objects toward each other without touching them. For example, Earth's gravity pulls objects toward the center of the planet. This constant pulling keeps objects on Earth's surface from flying off into space. It also causes objects to fall toward the ground.

Gravity is an important force of attraction between objects in the universe. Earth's gravity pulls on the moon, keeping the moon in orbit. The moon pulls on Earth, causing the tides. The sun pulls on Earth and the other planets, keeping them in its orbit. These objects in space do not touch, but the force of gravity affects them.

As important as gravity is, it is still simply a force that can be balanced and overcome by other forces. If you set a book on a table, gravity pulls down on the book. But the book does not fall to the ground, because the force of the table pushing up on the book is equal to the force of gravity. Remember that when forces are balanced, objects do not change their motion. When you throw a ball up into the air, the force of your throw is greater than the force of gravity, and so the ball goes upwards.

Magnets

Magnetism is another force that can act across a distance, without objects touching. When you hold a magnet near an object that contains iron, for example, the iron will be pulled toward the magnet. Only some materials are attracted to magnets.

Magnetic force also acts between magnets. Each magnet has a north and a south pole. The opposite poles of two magnets will be attracted, or pulled, toward one another. The north end of one magnet will be attracted to the south pole of another magnet. But two like poles—two north poles or two south poles—will push away from, or repel, each other.

Benchmark Review
SC.5.P.13.1

Student-Response Activity

❶ Which forces act on a tennis ball as it travels from one side of a tennis court to the other during a tennis match?

_____

_____

_____

_____

❷ A bowling ball is rolled down a bowling lane and knocks over several pins. Describe how the forces acting on the bowling ball and the pins affect their motion.

_____

_____

_____

_____

❸ Matt lined up the north pole of a magnet with the south pole of another magnet. Did the magnets attract or repel each other? Explain your answer.

_____

_____

_____

❹ Kiki and Jake both push on a box from opposite directions. At first, Kiki and Jake push the box with the same amount of force. Then Kiki pushes with 3 N of force and Jake pushes with 2 N. Describe what happens to the box.

_____

_____

_____

_____

Benchmark Assessment SC.5.P.13.1

Fill in the letter of the best choice.

❶ Which is **true** of gravity?

Ⓐ Gravity acts only through air, not through water or land.

Ⓑ Gravity does not act on airplanes flying in the sky.

Ⓒ Gravity always acts toward the center of Earth.

Ⓓ Gravity does not act on objects falling through space.

❷ Which forces can affect an object's motion without touching the object?

Ⓕ friction and gravity

Ⓖ gravity and magnetic force

Ⓗ friction and magnetic force

Ⓘ gravity, friction, and magnetic force

❸ Which describes how forces affect a soccer ball?

Ⓐ Forces cause it to change color and size.

Ⓑ Forces cause it to change speed and direction.

Ⓒ Forces cause it to change mass and position.

Ⓓ Forces cause it to change location and weight.

❹ If you held the object in the picture near paperclips containing iron, what would be the result?

Ⓕ The paper clips would be repelled.

Ⓖ The paper clips would be attracted.

Ⓗ The paper clips would not be affected.

Ⓘ The paper clips would be repelled by one pole and attracted to the other.

❺ Eli pushes a box with 1 N of force, and Judy pushes with 2 N in the opposite direction. Which describes what happens to the box?

Ⓐ It does not move.

Ⓑ It moves toward Eli.

Ⓒ It moves toward Judy.

Ⓓ It moves toward Eli and then toward Judy.

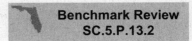
SC.5.P.13.2 Investigate and describe that the greater the force applied to it, the greater the change in motion of a given object.

Force, Mass, and Motion

Describing Motion

Motion is any change in the position of an object. An object's motion can be described by the distance the object traveled, by the direction it moved, and by how fast it traveled.

Speed is a measure of the distance an object moves over a certain amount of time. You can calculate speed by dividing the distance traveled by the time it took the object to travel that distance. If you apply a force in the same direction as the object is already moving, you will increase the speed of the object because the object will move the distance in a shorter time. If you apply a force in a different direction from the one in which the object is traveling, the force will cause the object the slow down, stop, or turn.

You can also describe the direction an object moves by using compass directions or words such as *up, down, left,* and *right* to indicate direction. When you tell both the speed and the direction of an object, you give its velocity. Two objects with the same speed have different velocities if they are moving in different directions.

Forces

A force is a push or pull. Forces can cause an object at rest to begin moving, or to change position. A force can cause an object in motion to change the way it is moving—stop, start, speed up, slow down, or turn. Any change in an object's velocity—its speed or direction—is called **acceleration**. So, forces cause acceleration.

Not all forces result in motion or acceleration. If equal forces act on an object in opposite directions, the forces are balanced. **Balanced forces** do not cause a change in motion. Only **unbalanced forces** affect an object's motion.

Force and Motion

Both the amount of force applied to an object and the direction of the force determine how the force will affect the motion of an object. If first a large force and then a small force act on the same object, the larger force will cause the object to move a greater distance and at a faster speed. If two forces act on an object from opposite directions, the object will move in the direction of the greater force.

Mass and Motion

The motion of an object is related to its mass. **Mass** is the amount of matter in an object. Consider pushing two objects of different masses with the same amount of force. The object with less mass will move a greater distance and at a higher speed. For example, if you push two toy cars with the same amount of force, the one with less mass will go faster and farther. If you push an empty shopping cart but keep adding groceries, you will have to push with greater and greater force to move at the same speed.

Benchmark Review
SC.5.P.13.2

Student-Response Activity

① Explain how the amount of force and an object's mass affect motion.

_____
_____
_____
_____

② Explain how balanced forces affect the motion of an object.

_____
_____
_____

③ Explain how unbalanced forces affect the motion of an object.

_____
_____
_____

④ Two runners run the same distance, but one runs in the morning and one runs in the evening. How could you determine which of the two runners ran the distance faster?

_____
_____
_____

Benchmark Assessment SC.5.P.13.2

Fill in the letter of the best choice.

❶ Which can **not** be changed by applying a force to an object?

Ⓐ mass

Ⓑ direction

Ⓒ speed

Ⓓ velocity

❷ The boy pulls a wagon.

What is likely to happen if the boy adds objects to the wagon?

Ⓕ He will find that it is easier to pull the wagon.

Ⓖ He will find that it is harder to pull the wagon.

Ⓗ He will find that he needs less force to pull the wagon.

Ⓘ He will find that he needs the same amount of force to pull the wagon.

❸ What do you need to know to find the speed of an object?

Ⓐ mass and position

Ⓑ distance and time

Ⓒ velocity and energy

Ⓓ force and mass

❹ What always changes when an object is in motion?

Ⓕ position

Ⓖ speed

Ⓗ direction

Ⓘ mass

❺ Dan plans to push several balls across a floor with the same amount of force. He will record data about distance each one traveled.

Ball	Mass	Distance
A	50 grams	
B	500 grams	
C	1 kilogram	
D	4 kilograms	

Which object do you predict will move the farthest?

Ⓐ A

Ⓑ B

Ⓒ C

Ⓓ D

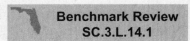
SC.3.L.14.1 Describe structures in plants and their roles in food production, support, water and nutrient transport, and reproduction.

What Are Some Plant Structures?

Plant Structures

Plants come in many shapes and sizes, but they all share similar structures that help them live and thrive. These parts include the roots, stem, leaves, flowers, and seeds. Each plant part has its own function, but together, they work together to ensure the plant can, grow survive and reproduce.

Roots

Roots anchor the plant in the soil. Roots also take in, or absorb, water and nutrients from the soil. **Nutrients** are materials that living things need to grow. Some roots can grow deep into the ground to reach water sources while others may stay shallow. Other roots have small, hairy branches that spread out to gather water from a large area. Water and nutrients move from the roots to other parts of the plant.

Stem

Water and nutrients move from the roots to the stem. The stem moves the water and nutrients from the roots to the parts of the plant above the ground. The stem also helps the plant stand tall and strong. The woody stems of trees grow dense and thick. The stems of flowers can be delicate and thin. Some plants have one stem, but others have many.

Leaves

Most plants make their own food. This process takes place in the plant's leaves. Leaves use air, water, and light energy from the sun to make its food. The food is then transported from the leaves through the stem to other parts of the plant. Plants use this food energy to live and grow. Leaves are many different sizes and shapes. Some plants have big, wide leaves that help it to catch sunlight.

Flowers and Seeds

The blossoms on apple trees and other plants are called flowers. A **flower** is the plant part that helps some plants reproduce. When living things **reproduce**, they make new living things like themselves.

During reproduction, one part of the flower develops into a fruit. After the fruit ripens, it falls to the ground. The fruit contains seeds. A seed contains a tiny, undeveloped plant, or embryo. A seed also has food for the embryo. Then sunlight, soil, water, and air help the seeds sprout into a seedling and grow into a new plant. This process is called the plant cycle of life. Some plants have cones instead of flowers, but like flowers, they reproduce by releasing seeds that are found in the cones.

Student-Response Activity

1 Identify each part of the plant. Describe the function of each part.

_____

_____

_____

_____

2 What are the steps in the life cycle of a peach tree?

_____

_____

_____

3 What are the three functions of a plant's stem?

_____

_____

_____

4 What is the difference between plant nutrients and food?

_____

_____

_____

Benchmark Assessment SC.3.L.14.1

Fill in the letter of the best choice.

❶ Which part produces food for the plant?

(A) flowers

(B) leaves

(C) roots

(D) seeds

❷ In the picture, what is the function of the part of the plant is the man holding?

(F) to make food

(G) to reproduce

(H) to move nutrients and water

(I) to hold the plant in the ground

❸ Which plant part is **not i**nvolved in its reproduction?

(A) seed

(B) flower

(C) fruit

(D) root

❹ What do the roots **not** provide for the plant?

(F) water

(G) food

(H) nutrients

(I) anchor into soil

❺ Which part of a plant cycle of life is shown in the picture?

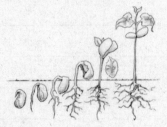

(A) seed growing into seedling

(B) blossom growing into fruit

(C) seedling growing into plant

(D) seed growing into fruit

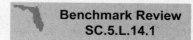
SC.5.L.14.1 Identify the organs in the human body and describe their functions, including the skin, brain, heart, lungs, stomach, liver, intestines, pancreas, muscles and skeleton, reproductive organs, kidneys, bladder, and sensory organs.

Organs and Organ Systems

Body Organization

An **organism** is a living thing. It is made of smaller parts that work together to meet its needs. An **organ** is a body part made up of even smaller parts that work together to do a certain job. Groups of organs work together. An **organ system** is a group of organs that do one type of job. Your body has several organ systems that help it meet your needs. All plants and animals are organisms that have organs and organ systems to meet their needs.

Nervous System

The job of the nervous system is to sense information about your environment and communicate within the body. The nervous system is made up of tiny structures called nerve cells. Collections of nerve cell fibers make up nerves that carry information to and from the spinal cord and brain. The brain is the organ that processes information and sends instructions to the body. It is made of millions of nerve cells working like a computer.

The spinal cord is a rope-like bundle of nerve cells and nerve fibers that runs along the backbone. It is the main pathway for information traveling to and from the brain. Some of the nerve fibers send information to the brain; others receive signals from the brain.

The brain receives and processes information collected by nerves in the eyes, ears, nose, and tongue. The brain decides on a response and sends messages through the spinal column. The spinal column directs the messages to nerves that connect to muscles. The messages tell the muscles what to do, such as telling the legs to run. This communication takes place in fractions of a second.

The Senses

Your senses are the body's way of collecting information about your environment. Special structures in parts of your body detect different things about the world around you.

Your eyes collect information as light enters the eye through a hole in the iris called the **pupil**. Light then passes through the lens and hits the back of the eye, or **retina**. In the retina, nerve cells detect light and send this information to the brain. The brain interprets the information as images that you see.

Your ears collect sound information that allows you to hear. The outer ear, the part of your ear that you can see, funnels sound into the middle ear. Sound causes the eardrum in the middle ear to vibrate. The vibrations are passed through tiny bones into the inner ear and into a fluid-filled structure called the **cochlea**. Nerves send messages about the vibrations to the brain, and you sense sound.

When you breath, air travels through your nose. Inside your nose are structures that sense chemicals in the air. These structures are attached to nerve cells in the olfactory bulb that send messages to the brain about the chemicals. This makes up your sense of smell.

The small bumps all over your tongue called taste buds are chemical detectors. They detect chemicals in things that enter the mouth.

Nerves attached to the taste buds send messages about the chemical to the brain. Your brain interprets these messages as taste.

Integumentary System

The function of the integumentary system is to protect the inside of your body and to help control body temperature. Your skin, hair, and nails are all parts of the integumentary system.

Skin protects your body by keeping germs out. It also helps keep water from leaving your body so you do not get dehydrated. The skin helps regulate body temperature through the release of sweat from sweat glands in the skin.

The nails protect the vulnerable ends of your fingers and toes from damage. Hair helps to cushion the body, protects it form the sun's damaging rays, and helps to keep the body warm.

The skin also has nerves that provide information about temperature, pressure, vibrations, and pain. Your sense of touch comes from nerves in the skin.

Skeletal System

The functions of the skeletal system are to support and protect the body and allow movement. The bones of the skull and the ribs protect the internal organs of the body. Bones attach to muscles to help move the body. Bones have a hard calcium-containing outer layer and a spongy inner layer from which blood cells are formed.

The place where two bones meet is called a joint. Some joints, such as those in the skull, do not allow bones to move. Other joints allow for different types of movement. Ligaments connect the bones of a joint.

Cartilage is a flexible material that cushions the ends of bones and forms the ends of ears and the nose. The skeletal system is made up of bones, cartilage, and ligaments.

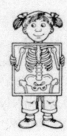

Muscular System

The major function of the muscular system is to produce movement in the body. **Muscles** are organs that contract to produce movement. Most muscles work in pairs. When one contracts to pull on bone, the other relaxes. Some muscle movements are involuntary; you do not have to control the beat of your heart. Other muscle movements, such as standing, are under your complete control.

There are three types of muscle. The heart is made of one type of muscle. A second type forms the walls of blood vessels and organs. The most abundant type is skeletal muscle that moves the bones.

Respiratory System

Organs in the respiratory system bring in oxygen that the body needs and release carbon dioxide, the body's waste gas. The main organs of the respiratory system are the lungs.

Air brought into the body through the nose and mouth travels through the trachea to the two bronchi. The bronchi branch into smaller vessels called bronchioles. At the end of each bronchiole are tiny air sacs called alveoli. The alveoli are surrounded by capillaries.

Oxygen diffuses from the alveoli into the blood in the capillaries. At the same time, waste carbon dioxide in the blood diffuses into the alveoli. The carbon dioxide is then exhaled out of the body.

Circulatory System

The circulatory system pumps oxygen and nutrients throughout the body and helps to remove waste. The components of the circulatory system are the heart, the blood vessels, and blood.

Blood is made up of a clear liquid called plasma containing cells and nutrients. Blood contains cells in three main types: white cells, red cells, and platelets. Red blood cells carry oxygen throughout the body. White blood cells help fight disease. Platelets help stop bleeding by forming clots.

The human heart has four chambers—two top and two bottom chambers. The top chambers contract to push blood into the bottom chambers. The bottom chambers then contract to push the blood out of the heart. The blood travels through the vessels.

There are three main types of blood vessels. Arteries carry blood away from the heart. Arteries branch and get smaller until they are tiny vessels called capillaries. Nutrients and gases can transfer between the capillaries and tissue. Blood is returned to the heart through veins.

Digestive System

The digestive system breaks food down into nutrients for the body. The organs of the digestive system include the esophagus, the stomach, and the small and large intestines. In addition, the liver, pancreas, and gallbladder play roles in digestion.

Food moves from the mouth to the stomach through the esophagus. In the stomach, acids and the churning of the stomach muscles turn the food into liquid. The food enters the small intestine, where digestive juices made in the pancreas and liver help break down fats and proteins. The nutrients are then absorbed in the small intestine. The remaining food materials pass into the large intestine, where water and minerals are absorbed. The solid waste then leaves the body.

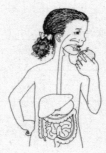

Excretory System

The excretory system eliminates waste that comes from body functions. The structures of the excretory system are the kidneys, ureters, bladder, and urethra.

The use of nutrients to produce energy in the cells leaves toxic waste products behind, such as carbon dioxide and ammonia. The carbon dioxide is exhaled out of the body. The other waste products are filtered from the

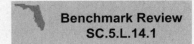
blood by the kidneys. The resulting urine travels through the ureters to the bladder. The urine is stored in the bladder until it passes from the body through the urethra.

In addition to filtering the blood, the kidneys help to control the water and salt balance of the body.

Reproductive System

The job of the reproductive system is to make new organisms. The reproductive cells of human males, the sperm, are made in the testes. The reproductive cells of human females, the eggs, are made in the ovaries. These special cells join to form the human embryo. The embryo develops and grows inside the mother. When the baby is ready to live outside the mother, it is born.

Student-Response Activity

1 Describe the primary functions of each organ in the human body.

heart _____

_____

small intestine _____

_____

bone _____

_____

nose _____

_____

kidney _____

_____

brain _____

_____

Name ______________________________ Date ____________

Benchmark Review
SC.5.L.14.1

2. Describe how the circulatory and respiratory systems work together to exchange oxygen and waste carbon dioxide.

____
____
____
____
____
____

3. Explain the sequence of events that would allow you to catch a ball thrown toward you?

____
____
____
____
____
____

Benchmark Assessment SC.5.L.14.1

Fill in the letter of the best choice.

❶ Which does not play a role in digestion?

Ⓐ ovaries

Ⓑ pancreas

Ⓒ small intestine

Ⓓ stomach

❷ Which structure sends information about vibrations to the brain?

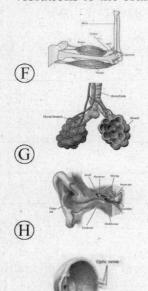

Ⓕ

Ⓖ

Ⓗ

Ⓘ

❸ Which statement about the skin is **false**?

Ⓐ It helps prevent infection.

Ⓑ It helps absorb nutrients.

Ⓒ It helps regulate body temperature.

Ⓓ It helps prevent water loss.

❹ Which is the correct sequence of signals in the nervous system?

Ⓕ eye → nerve → brain → spinal column → muscle

Ⓖ eye → brain → spinal column → nerve → muscle.

Ⓗ muscle → nerve → spinal column → brain → eye

Ⓘ muscle → brain → spinal column → nerve → eye

❺ Human cells need oxygen and produce carbon dioxide waste. Which depicts the system that exchanges these gases between the body and the air?

Ⓐ   Ⓒ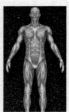

Ⓑ 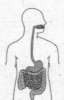   Ⓓ

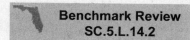
SC.5.L.14.2 Compare and contrast the function of organs and other physical structures of plants and animals, including humans, for example: some animals have skeletons for support – some with internal skeletons others with exoskeletons – while some plants have stems for support.

Comparing Structures of Plants and Animals

Sensory Structures

All organisms have sensory structures that help them survive. The human eye has a single lens that focuses light on the retina for vision. Some organisms, like the fly, have a compound eye that has thousands of lenses

The human ear sends sound information to the brain for hearing. Bats and dolphins are examples of animals that send out sound waves in order to navigate and find food. The sound that bounces off objects and returns to their ears helps them "see" in the dark.

Many animals detect chemicals on internal structures in the nose and mouth. Moths detect chemicals on their external antennae.

Plants get information from the environment, too. Some plants have sensitive hairs that provide information to the plant. In the Venus flytrap, hairs will signal the leaves to close when they are triggered.

Body Coverings

All bodies have some type of outer coverings. Skin, nails, and bits of hair protect the human body, retain water, and regulate temperature. Many animals have a much more extensive covering of hair or fur on their bodies. Other animals have scales. Birds are covered in feathers that help them fly and regulate temperature. Some animals have hard shells over all or parts of their bodies.

Plants also have body coverings. Trees have hard and thick bark that protects the inner part of the plant. Many plants have a waxy coating on their stems and leaves to prevent water loss.

Support and Movement

Like humans, animals and plants have systems that support their bodies and allow them to move. Unlike humans, not all animals have their support on the inside. Insects have a hard outer covering called an exoskeleton that provides protection and aids in movement. Just as human muscles are connected to bones for movement, insect muscles are connected to the exoskeleton. However, unlike bones, the exoskeleton does not grow with the insect. It is shed and a new one underneath hardens.

Many animals have special structures for movement in specific environments. Animals that live underwater have fins, flippers, and flukes to help them move through water.

Plants, particularly tall ones, need support. Thick, woody stems help support plants. Even though plants do not move to different locations, many do move in place. Some plants have sensitive leaves that open or close in response to touch or to a change in light. Plants may also move to face the light.

Respiration and Circulation

All animals must take in oxygen and get it to all the cells in their body—they just do not all do it the same way. Fish spend all their time under water and do not have lungs. Instead, they use their gills to extract oxygen from water. Spiders have a structure called a book lung that has flat sheets of tissue that fill with air. Because birds need a lot of oxygen for flight, they have air sacs that store air so that it is always available, even when they exhale. Plants take in air to obtain carbon dioxide, which they use to make food. Plants have a leaf structure called a stoma that opens and closes to control the passage of air.

Whatever structure an animal has to take in air, oxygen is passed from it to the blood in the circulation. Some animals have two- or three-chambered hearts, rather than the four chambers a human heart has. Plants do not have blood, but nutrients and gases are dissolved in water that is transported around the plant in vessels.

Digestion and Excretion

All organisms take in nutrients and eliminate waste. Living things have many ways of doing this. Animal mouth parts vary widely. Some insects have straw-like mouth parts that suck up liquids. Digestion starts in the mouth of humans and many animals. Other animals release digestive enzymes outside their bodies before they take in food. Animals that eat fibrous plants chew their food more than once. Others have stomachs with multiple sections.

Some animals, like the tapeworm, do not have digestive systems of their own and absorb nutrients from their surroundings instead. Plants also take in nutrients from their surroundings.

Humans excrete solid, liquid, and gas waste. Birds do not excrete liquid urine. They excrete uric acid along with their solid waste. Some animals, such as jellyfish, do not have a separate excretory pathway. These animals eliminate waste through their mouths. Even plants eliminate waste. Oxygen and, in some plants, excess salt are released by the leaves.

Reproduction

In humans, and many animals, the new organism grows and develops inside the mother. Other animals lay eggs outside the mother. The embryo grows inside the egg and then hatches from the egg. Some organisms have direct development where the young looks like a smaller version of the adult. In other organisms, the young do not look like the adult and must go through developmental stages of metamorphosis to mature. Insects hatch from the egg as larvae and go through stages before reaching adulthood. Frogs are born as tadpoles with tails but no legs. As they grow, they develop legs and lose the tails until they look like adult frogs.

Plants have a variety of reproductive strategies. Most plants form seeds, whether in flowers or cones, that develop into new plants. Some plants reproduce through spores. Many plants are also able to reproduce from cuttings of the mature plant.

Student-Response Activity

❶ How is the reproduction of a frog like the reproduction of a plant?

_____

_____

_____

_____

❷ Describe three ways animals obtain oxygen differently from humans.

_____

_____

_____

_____

❸ How is plant movement different from animal movement?

_____

_____

_____

❹ Explain how these pairs of structures are related.

a. moth antennae / human nose _____

b. apple seed / chicken egg _____

c. hawk feathers / monkey fur _____

d. sunflower stem / elephant bones _____

Benchmark Assessment SC.5.L.14.2

Fill in the letter of the best choice.

1 Which structures have similar functions?

(A) gills / veins

(B) bark / bone

(C) antennae / tongue

(D) feathers / fins

2 Which is **not** a correct statement about insects?

(F) They have their skeletons on the outside of their bodies.

(G) Their eyes may have thousands of lenses.

(H) They absorb nutrients through their skin

(I) They lay eggs to reproduce.

3 Which of the following organisms takes in oxygen through book lungs?

(A)

(B)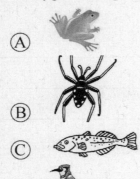

(C)

(D)

4 Which is a way digestion in some animals differs from humans?

(F) Acids break down food.

(G) Nutrients are absorbed through the skin.

(H) Food is broken down by chewing.

(I) Food is digested in the stomach.

5 Which describes the dolphin sense depicted?

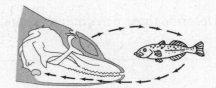

(A) The dolphin smells chemicals coming from the fish.

(B) The dolphin hears sound waves made by movement of the fish.

(C) The dolphin sees light reflecting off the fish.

(D) The dolphin detects sound bouncing back from the fish.

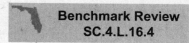
SC.4.L.16.4 Compare and contrast the major stages in the life cycles of Florida plants and animals, such as those that undergo incomplete and complete metamorphosis, and flowering and nonflowering seed-bearing plants.

Life Cycles of Plants and Animals

What Is a Life Cycle?

Every living thing has a **life cycle**, or a series of changes that occur during its life. An organism's life cycle begins when it is born, hatches, or germinates. The organism grows and reaches adulthood or maturity. Eventually, all organisms die. The life cycle will continue, though, as long as the adults reproduced and their young survive.

Plant Life Cycles

Plants can be classified in two into two groups: those that produce seeds and those that do not. Most plants produce seeds. **Seeds** are the structures containing a tiny, undeveloped plant called an embryo that has started to grow inside. The hard outer covering of the seed, called the seed coat, protects the embryo. Seeds also have stored food for the embryo to use when the seed **germinates**, or begins to grow.

Mosses and ferns do not produce seeds. They produce spores. Like a seed, a spore will grow into a new plant. However, spores do not have an embryo inside, and they do not contain much stored food.

The fern life cycle is very complex. Spores develop on the underside of an adult ferns leaves. When a spore is released and lands on moist soil, it grows into a small, heart-shaped form from which an adult fern develops.

Flowering Plants

Flowering plants start life as a seed. Inside the seed, the embryo is dormant. It uses very little energy, and it is not growing. When the temperature and moisture are right, the seed germinates. A small root and stem start to grow. A small plant that has just started to grow is called a **seedling**. The plant continues to grow more roots, stems, and leaves. This is called the vegetative stage.

The next stage in a plant's life cycle is called a mature plant. At this time, the plant begins to make flowers. Flowers produce pollen. In order for new seeds to form, pollen must travel from one part of a flower to another. For many plants, bees carry pollen from one plant to another. In some plants, a fruit grows from part of the pollinated flower. Seeds develop inside the fruit, and the cycle starts again.

Cone-Bearing Plants

Some plants produce seeds without using flowers. These plants have cones instead. **Conifers,** which include pine trees, are one type of cone-bearing plants.

A seed contains an embryo. When conditions are just right, the seed germinates. It grows and becomes a seedling. The seedling grows into a mature, or adult, tree.

Male cones produce pollen. Wind carries the pollen to the female cones. Seeds develop in the female cones, and the life cycle continues.

Animal Life Cycles

There are many variations in animal life cycles. Some young look very similar to the adults they will become. Other young do not look like adults of their species. They change drastically as they grow and develop.

When an animal goes through a change in body form as part of its life cycle, it is called **metamorphosis**. During metamorphosis, new body parts form. This change occurs as a young animal develops into an adult animal. Often, the young eat a different food source than the adults.

Frogs

Frogs start their lives in eggs. In the egg, a tadpole develops. When it hatches, it has a mouth, gills, and a tail. The tadpole sticks to the underside of a plant until it has grown more of a body and then begins to swim like a fish.

Metamorphosis begins after about six weeks. Tiny legs start to grow, and then tiny arms begin to grow. It looks like a frog with a long tail. By the twelfth week, the tail is absorbed into the body. The tadpole is now a small frog. Adult frogs have lungs and must breathe air. They can live on land, but their skin must stay moist.

Butterflies and Ladybugs

Butterflies and ladybugs are insects that change during their life cycles. Although they do not look alike, butterflies and ladybugs go through the same stages in their life cycles.

Both life cycles begin with an egg. When the egg hatches, a worm-like **larva** crawls out. Larvae eat a lot of food. Butterfly larvae, called caterpillars, eat leaves, Ladybug larvae eat tiny insects such as mites and aphids. As the larvae grow, they shed their skin several times.

Eventually, the larva will stop growing and attach itself to a leaf. It changes into a **pupa**. Inside the pupa, metamorphosis occurs. The organism grows wings and other new body parts. Its shape changes and it becomes an adult.

Adult butterflies no longer have mouthparts for chewing. Instead they sip nectar from flowers with their straw-like mouths. Adult ladybugs have a hard shell with wings underneath it. When adults reproduce, the female lays eggs and the life cycle begins again.

Chickens

Many animals, including birds, mammals, fish, and reptiles, do not undergo metamorphosis during their life cycle. In these animals, young are born live or hatch from an egg. The young have the same body form as the adults. The young grow and develop continuously and slowly become adults. When animals mature in this way, it is called **direct development**.

Chickens undergo direct development. The life cycle begins when an adult female lays a fertilized egg. Inside the egg, an embryo is developing. The chick hatches, and it has all the body parts of an adult. Each day, it grows and develops a little more. Eventually, it matures and becomes an adult. Adults can reproduce.

Student-Response Activity

❶ Use the terms in the word bank to label the life cycle stages for each organism.

Word Bank

seedling   mature plant   larva   tadpole   egg   adult   pupa

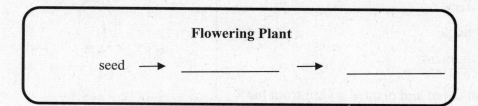

Flowering Plant

seed → _____ → _____

Ladybug

_____ → _____ → _____ → adult

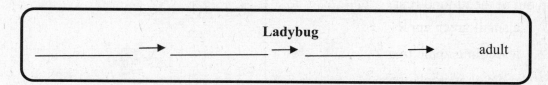

Frog

egg → _____ → _____

❷ Some plants have flowers. Why are flowers important in the life cycle of some plants?

_____

_____

_____

_____

❸ How does the life cycle of a chicken differ from the life cycle of a frog?

_____

_____

_____

_____

Benchmark Assessment SC.4.L.16.4

Fill in the letter of the best choice.

1 Which organism undergoes metamorphosis?

Ⓐ ladybug

Ⓑ fern

Ⓒ eagle

Ⓓ humans

2 Jonah saved and planted a seed from his apple. What might he expect to see come up out of the ground first?

Ⓕ a small green apple

Ⓖ a seedling apple tree

Ⓗ roots of an apple tree

Ⓘ a mature apple tree

3 Which is a young frog that will turn into an adult?

Ⓐ

Ⓑ

Ⓒ

Ⓓ

4 A moth and a ladybug undergo the same life cycle stages. Which stage comes after a moth's pupa stage?

Ⓕ

Ⓖ

Ⓗ

Ⓘ

5 When a caterpillar becomes a pupa, what happens inside?

Ⓐ It hibernates.

Ⓑ It grows different organs and wings.

Ⓒ It rests and comes out just the same.

Ⓓ It comes out the same shape, but smaller since it couldn't eat.

SC.5.L.17.1 Compare and contrast adaptations displayed by animals and plants that enable them to survive in different environments such as life cycles variations, animal behaviors and physical characteristics.

What Is Adaptation?

Adapting to Habitat

Animals and plants live in varied conditions around the world. The place where a living thing lives is called a **habitat**. There are many types of habitats. A living thing must be able to meet its needs within its habitat, which also means that some animals may be able to survive only within their habitat. For example, plants and animals that live in the desert will probably not survive in a rain forest. The characteristic that helps a living thing survive is called an **adaptation**. If this characteristic is key to its survival in a habitat that does not change, it will be passed down over generations resulting in a thriving population in that habitat.

Physical Adaptations

Some adaptations are differences in the bodies of plants and animals. These are called physical adaptations. Some physical adaptations can help living things from being eaten. For example, sharp thorns keep a plant's stems from being eaten. Another physical adaptation helps keep an animal hidden. This adaptation, called camouflage, is the ability for an animal to blend in to its surroundings. Other physical adaptations help animals hunt, such as keen eyesight and sharp talons on an eagle. Plants also have adaptations, such as edible fruit or fragrant flowers that help them reproduce by spreading seeds or distributing pollen.

Behavior Adaptations

Behaviors that animals know how to do without being taught are called **instincts**. Spiders do not have to be taught to spin webs and baby sea turtles know to return to the water after hatching. Migration is an instinctive behavior in which animals move to different locations at certain times of the year to find food, reproduce, or escape cold weather. Hibernation is another instinctive behavior in response to changes to seasons. It is a long period of inactivity when an animal's body processes slow down. Behavior adaptations also may have a social purpose, seen in the "waggle dance" of bees that communicate information to the hive such as direction to go for food, how far away, or even what kind of food it is. Other behaviors that have to be taught are called learned behaviors. For example, a lion has to teach its cub how to hunt prey.

Life Cycle Adaptations

The life cycle of a living thing goes through multiple stages, and differences in life cycles are adaptations to habitat. An example of a life cycle adaptation is seen with tadpoles and frogs. Upon hatching, tadpoles have to live in water. In areas where water dries quickly, the tadpole's development into a frog is faster than in environments where water is abundant. An adult frog can live on land and eats different food. As an adaptation, this helps frogs survive, as tadpoles and adults don't have to compete for the same food source.

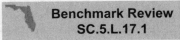
Adaptations to Life on Land

Temperate forests have wide leaves that block a lot of sunlight. Plants that live beneath these trees are adapted to live with less light. Vines climb the tree to reach the light. Many animals that live in these forests have adaptations that allow them to climb or live in trees. The birds have feet that help them perch on branches, and the insects have mouth parts that let them bore into wood. In the fall, the trees lose their leaves to prevent water loss from the dry winter air.

Tropical rain forests are warm and rainy all year. Two layers of trees block a lot of the sunlight from reaching the ground. In this third layer, plants live close to the ground and have adapted to low light levels. The soil in the tropical forests is very thin, so trees have special root systems that keep them from falling over. Animals also have adaptations that help them live in the forest. A howler monkey's loud voice allows it to be heard a long way away. Some animals, like jaguars, have claws that help it climb trees and hunt. Others, like sloths, have strong arms and claws that help them hang from trees.

In the **grasslands**, there are few trees and frequent fires. The grasses' long, narrow leaves help them keep from losing very much water, and their large root system helps them grow back quickly after fires. The plant eaters have flat teeth that help them chew grass. Many animals are very fast, for either hunting or escaping. With few places to hide, some small animals live underground in burrows. Keen eyesight helps eagles and vultures spot their prey from above.

Plants that live in the **desert**, like cacti, have thick bodies that can store a lot of water. Waxy coatings and small leaves help keep water from escaping. Many desert animals are nocturnal, so they sleep in the hot day, and come out for the cooler nights. Camels have wide feet for walking on sand. They can also close their nostrils during a wind storm to keep sand out of their lungs.

In the **taiga**, conifer trees are common. These trees are evergreens, but they grow seeds inside of hard cones that withstand harsh weather. Their pointed tops and flexible branches keep them from breaking under the weight of snow and ice. The animals have thick fur that protects them from the cold. Many of the birds migrate in the fall to escape the cold winters.

In the **tundra**, plants grow and reproduce in the few months when the ground is not frozen. In other **polar** regions, plants do not grow at all. Plant-like organisms called lichens survive on the rocks, and some animals eat them. Many animals are camouflaged by white fur or feathers. Thick layers of fat and water-proof feathers help the penguin survive the frigid winter.

Adaptations to Life on Water

Ponds and **lakes** are freshwater habitats that are divided into zones. The zone closest to shore has many living things in it. Plants grow in the shallow parts where the roots can reach bottom and the leaves can get enough sunlight. Further away from shore, only floating plants can grow. In the deepest zone, there is no light, so plants cannot grow. The catfish, worms, and bacteria that live there feed off dead plants and animals that fall from above.

In a **river** or **stream**, the water is constantly moving, and the faster it moves, the harder it is for living things to survive. Plants tend to grow near the banks, and mosses have hair-like structures that help them cling to rocks. Fish constantly swim upstream to not be carried away by the current.

The **wetlands** plants have special tissues that carry air from the plant's leaves to its roots. If the marsh is near the ocean, plants also have adaptations to get rid of excess salt. Home to many plants and animals, the wetlands also serve as rest areas for migrating water birds. A heron's long legs blend in with the reeds, and an alligator's raised eyes and nostrils help it hide in shallow water while hunting.

The **intertidal zone** is where the ocean meets the land. It is constantly being struck by waves. Every day, the tide comes in and covers the zone with salt water. After the tide goes out, the zone is exposed to air and sunlight. Living things here have adaptations to protect their bodies from being crushed, washed away, or dried out.

The largest habitat, the **ocean**, is divided into zones. The top zone, the photic zone, receives light, so seaweed and other plantlike organisms can use sun to make food. Colorful fish blend in to the coral reefs. The next zone, the aphotic zone, is dark and cold. Some animals move between these layers. Living things at the ocean floor may depend on the heat and minerals from deep-sea vents. Their bodies are adapted to living under great pressure, and most cannot survive closer to the surface.

Student-Response Activity

❶ For each type of adaptation—physical, behavioral and life cycle— provide an example and explain how the adaptation is suitable for its habitat.

physical _____

_____

behavioral _____

_____

life cycle _____

_____

❷ Classify each behavioral adaptation.

Geese flying south for the winter _____

Monkeys grooming each other _____

Horse walking within hours of birth _____

Tiger cubs on first hunt _____

Bears sleeping in den through winter _____

Beavers building dams _____

❸ Describe the physical adaptations for ducks and cacti and how the adaptations helps
them live in their respective habitats.

_____

_____

_____

_____

❹ Identify a plant and animal that are adapted for the swamplands of the Florida Everglades
and how their adaptations would prohibit them from surviving in the Nevada desert.

_____

_____

_____

_____

Benchmark Assessment SC.5.L.17.1

Fill in the letter of the best choice.

❶ What is **not** an adaptation due to life cycle?

(A) ability to alter birth time due to environment

(B) separate environments and food sources for different life cycle phases

(C) a lioness protecting its cub

(D) short bloom and seed reproduction cycle triggered only when it rains

❷ The camel's hump is example of what type of adaptation?

(F) physical

(G) instinct

(H) life cycle

(I) learned behavior

❸ What physical characteristic is an adaptation for an animal that hunts?

(A) sharp teeth and claws

(B) gills on a fish

(C) hanging upside down to sleep

(D) webbed feet

❹ What adaptation does a black bear have that could help it survive in the tundra?

(F) dark fur

(G) flat teeth for crushing acorns and nuts

(H) a thick coat

(I) curved claws for climbing trees

❺ Which adaptation would help an organism survive in the intertidal zone?

(A) dries out quickly in the sun

(B) suction cups

(C) soft body shell

(D) waterproof feathers

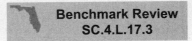
SC.4.L.17.3 Trace the flow of energy from the Sun as it is transferred along the food chain through the producers to the consumers.

What Is a Food Chain?

What Is a Food Chain?

A **food chain** is the transfer of food energy in a sequence of living things. The sun is the source of energy in most food chains. Producers are the next link in the food chain. **Producers** are living things that can make their own food. For example, algae grow in a pond and use the sun's energy to make their own food. It is the first link in a food chain.

Consumers cannot make their own food. They must eat other living things. The next link in the example chain is the mosquito larvae that eat the algae. To continue the food chain, minnows eat the larvae, larger fish eat the minnows, and people can then catch and eat the fish.

Another example of a food chain starts with the sun and then grass, the producer. A grasshopper eats the grass, and a frog eats the grasshopper. A snake eats the frog, and a hawk eats the snake.

Consumers in a Food Chain

Consumers can be placed into groups by the type of food they eat. **Herbivores** eat only grasses and other plants. **Carnivores** eat only other animals. Omnivores eat both plants and animals. Consumers that eat dead plants and animals are called **scavengers**.

Predator versus Prey

Consumers can also be grouped by whether they hunt or are hunted. A **predator** is an animal that hunts other animals. An animal that is eaten is the **prey**. Some animals can be predator or prey.

Food Webs

A food chain shows how energy moves from one living thing to another. Since consumers often eat a variety of foods, a single food chain does not fully describe the food energy relationships. A **food web** shows the relationships among different food chains.

Changes in Food Webs

Food webs show how complex the relationship between food chains can be. One small change can affect the entire food web. Consider an extended drought that dried up normally flowing creeks and tributaries. Without water in the area, small prey that depend on the water, plant life, and fish will move to another area or perish, thereby decreasing the predator population as well.

Student-Response Activity

❶ Describe the classification of each consumer in the list below.

herbivore _____

carnivore _____

omnivore _____

predator _____

prey _____

❷ Arrange the following in a food chain: hawk, frog, grass, snake, sun, grasshopper.

_____

_____

❸ Classify these animals as predator or prey.

_____   _____   _____   _____

❹ Describe the potential impact to the food webs in a desert region if most plants were killed by disease.

_____

_____

_____

_____

_____

_____

Benchmark Assessment SC.4.L.17.3

Fill in the letter of the best choice.

1 The animal in the picture is an example of what consumer classification?

- (A) herbivore
- (B) predator
- (C) scavenger
- (D) prey

2 If a consumer eats other animals, which classification does **not** apply?

- (F) prey
- (G) omnivore
- (H) carnivore
- (I) predator

3 Complete the following food chain:
algae → tadpoles → **?** → hawk

- (A) minnows
- (B) bear
- (C) fish
- (D) water lilies

4 Which classification does not apply to this animal?

- (F) prey
- (G) carnivore
- (H) predator
- (I) omnivore

5 Which is **true** about food webs?

- (A) Food webs are a model consisting of multiple food chains.
- (B) Food webs are not affected by environmental changes.
- (C) Scavengers don't affect food webs because they only eat dead animals or plants.
- (D) Food webs aren't affected by a change in a single food chain.

FSSA Practice Test–Form A

Instructions–Form A

The following pages contain a practice test. Do not look at the test until your teacher tells you to begin.

Use the answer sheet on page 137 to mark your answers.

Read each question carefully. Restate the question in your own words.

Watch for key words such as *not*, *most*, and *least*.

A question might include one or more tables, graphs, diagrams, or pictures. Study these carefully before choosing an answer.

For questions 1–60, find the best answer. Fill in the answer bubble for that answer. Do not make any stray marks around answer spaces.

FSSA Practice Test–Form A

DIRECTIONS
Read each question carefully. Determine the best answer to the question from the answer choices provided. Then fill in the answer on your answer sheet.

1 Which part of this food chain uses light energy from the sun?

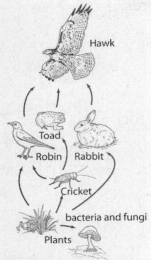

Hawk
Toad
Robin Rabbit
Cricket
bacteria and fungi
Plants
Dead plant or animal

  A the hawk, because it has plenty of prey

  B the dead leaves, because decomposers eat them

  C the green plants, because they produce food for crickets

  D the birds, because sunlight helps them find insects and seeds

2 In which galaxy is Earth found?

  F Andromeda

  G Crab Nebula

  H Orion

  I The Milky Way

3 Which is an adaptation of behavior that helps an animal survive?

  A A barn owl hears mice moving through grass at night.

  B A chimpanzee fishes for termites with a stick.

  C A polar bear's thick fur keeps it warm in Arctic winters.

  D A duck's webbed feet paddle on a freshwater pond.

4 Which organ of a species works **most like** a human skeleton?

  F a polar bear's fur

  G a giraffe's neck

  H a lobster's shell

  I a fish's scales

5 Luisa wants to make plastic from banana peels. She mixes more than a dozen compounds to make her plastic. On her fourth try, she successfully produces a thin, waterproof coating. Kevin and Jun follow her science notes and use the same quantities of each material. Neither student is able to reproduce the plastic that Luisa made. Which is a fair evaluation of Luisa's experiment?

A The experiment is a success because Luisa produced a thin, waterproof plastic.

B The experiment is not a success because the plastic cannot be reproduced by others.

C The experiment is a success because Kevin and Jun probably did not follow Luisa's directions.

D The experiment is not a success because Luisa wrote poor notes.

6 Which animal species has a life cycle that compares **most closely** to that of Florida Key deer?

F a crocodile

G a loggerhead turtle

H a manatee

I a wood stork

7 What function do these organs have in the human body?

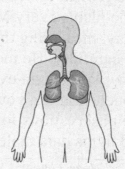

A intake of oxygen and removal of waste gas from the body

B processing and use of nutrients from food

C allowing motion of arms and legs

D experience of the five senses

8 What does this illustration represent?

F asteroid belt

G galaxy

H solar system

I star

9 Josh is doing an experiment to find out how different amounts of water affect the growth of bean plants. He waters the plants every Monday and Friday, measuring the amount of water carefully. He measures the change in plant height every Friday. What conclusion can you draw from the observations Josh recorded in his data table?

Plant	Water provided	Week 1	Week 2	Week 3	Week 4
Plant 1	2 mL	No growth	1 cm	2 cm	3 cm
Plant 2	6 mL	No growth	2 cm	4 cm	8 cm
Plant 3	12 mL	1 cm	5 cm	9 cm	16 cm
Plant 4	24 mL	No growth	No growth	No growth	No growth

A Plants 1, 2, and 3 showed successful growth.

B Plant 2 and 3 will produce nearly the same number of beans.

C Plant 3 received an amount of water that encouraged rapid growth.

D Plant 4 should have grown the most. There was a problem with the seed.

10 In this illustration, which types of energy are produced?

F heat and light

G light and mechanical

H mechanical and heat

I sound and light

11 Look at the diagram. Which step in the water cycle is missing?

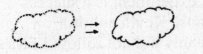

A condensation into clouds

B evaporation into water vapor

C precipitation in the form of rain

D runoff of rain into a lake

12 Which answer is an example of a pull changing motion?

  F picking up a bucket of apples

  G rolling a bowling ball down an alley

  H squashing a footprint into sand

  I using a finger to ring a doorbell

13 The crate is too large and heavy for the man to move it. How can he get it to move?

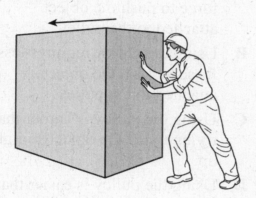

  A He can pull from the other side.

  B He can reduce the amount of force applied to the crate.

  C He turn the crate on its side and push.

  D He can get help to increase the force to move the crate.

14 A 10-meter high sand dune forms in a desert. What **most likely** caused this?

  F changing tides

  G chemical weathering

  H erosion by wind

  I intense flooding

15 Which structure functions to protect an organism within its environment?

  A beak shape on a flamingo

  B eye color of a panther

  C quills on a porcupine

  D tail on a cat

16 Which is **most like** the movement of blood in a human being?

  F Heat from the sun warms an alligator, and that warmth spreads throughout the body.

  G Water enters gills of a fish, and oxygen is taken out of the water.

  H Food is eaten by a bear, and the nutrients are used in all muscle structures.

  I Water enters plant roots and travels through the stem and leaves.

17 Students are studying minerals in class. Which property of a mineral can be determined using this equipment?

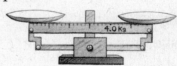

  A density

  B magnetism

  C mass

  D volume

18 Which object in a solar system orbits a planet?

  F asteroid

  G comet

  H meteor

  I moon

19 The map shows air temperatures and a warm front. How is this information used?

  A to record precipitation

  B to track a hurricane

  C to change the weather

  D to predict the weather in a city

20 Rachelle falls in a muddy puddle. Which body organ protects her from the organisms living in the puddle?

  F lungs

  G muscles

  H skeleton

  I skin

21 How does this simple machine work?

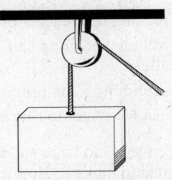

  A Using the pulley requires more force to push the object attached to the pulley.

  B Using the pulley requires less force to push the object attached to the pulley.

  C Using the pulley is harder than trying to lift the object straight up.

  D Using the pulley is easier than trying to lift the object straight up.

22 Into what form of energy does this appliance convert electrical energy?

  F mechanical energy

  G potential energy

  H sound energy

  I thermal energy

23 Which group contains only renewable resources?

A water, wind, and coal

B plant matter, oil, and solar power

C petroleum, natural gas, and water

D sun, wind, and plant matter

24 Students plan experiments for growing grass. Which environment will most likely grow grass?

F a planter covered with thin, black plastic

G a planter covered by aluminum foil

H a planter placed in a clear, one-gallon plastic bag

I a planter placed under a bamboo screen

25 Which gets its food by tapping into tree trunks and taking out insects hiding under the bark?

A

B

C

D

26 How could you separate this mixture?

F by color

G by a magnet

H by shape and color

I by size

27 Which model **best** represents Earth's movement that results in what we know as day and night?

A a skier going down a mountain

B an ice skater spinning in a tight circle

C a tennis ball hit by a racket

D an arrow shot through the air

Use this diagram to answer questions 28 and 29.

28 Which change in the this set-up would reduce the amount of pull needed to move the cart up the ramp?

F remove two books to change the angle of the ramp

G change the ramp for a shorter ramp

H increase the mass of the cart

I increase the length of the wire used to pull the cart

29 A student applies a force to the cart to pull it up the ramp. Which other force acting on the cart might slow its motion?

A gravity

B mechanical energy

C a push from behind the cart

D increased mass

30 Kara has several mineral samples without labels. She knows only one sample contains iron. Which physical property would **best** help her determine which sample contains iron?

F magnetism

G particle size

H shape

I streak

31 Which describes a liquid?

A has no volume

B has particles that are fairly rigid and fixed in place

C does not have mass that can be measured

D takes the shape of its container

32 A piece of mica breaks apart along even planes, producing smooth surfaces. Which property of minerals does this show?

F cleavage

G hardness

H luster

I texture

33 Which two human body systems does this illustration show?

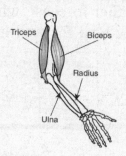

- **A** muscular and circulatory
- **B** nervous and skeletal
- **C** respiratory and circulatory
- **D** skeletal and muscular

34 Which step in the water cycle represents water changing from liquid to gas?

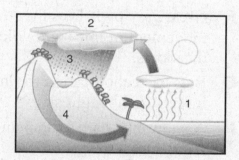

- **F** 1
- **G** 2
- **H** 3
- **I** 4

35 Which correctly orders these space objects from smallest to largest?

- **A** planets, moons, asteroids, comets
- **B** galaxies, stars, solar systems, planets
- **C** asteroids, planets, solar systems, galaxies
- **D** moon, planets, meteors, stars

36 Which is an example of kinetic energy?

- **F** a soccer ball lying on the grass
- **G** a swing hanging from a tree branch
- **H** a car parked in a driveway
- **I** a tennis ball bouncing against a wall

37 Which event occurs after one complete rotation of Earth?

- **A** a change from one day to the next day
- **B** a change from one month to another month
- **C** a change of summer to fall
- **D** a change from one year to the next year

38 What is the amount of matter in a solid, liquid, or gas called?

- **F** mass
- **G** temperature
- **H** texture
- **I** volume

39 A campfire burns and leaves ash behind. What causes the ash?

- **A** a chemical change
- **B** a physical change
- **C** a chemical property
- **D** a physical property

40 Which item in a solar system produces the **most** energy and gravitational pull?

F comet

G moon

H planet

I sun

Use this diagram to answer questions 41 and 42.

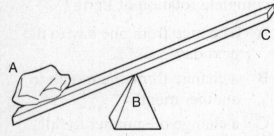

41 Which type of energy makes this simple machine work?

A chemical energy

B electrical energy

C light energy

D mechanical energy

42 Which type of force will cause the position of the rock to change?

F a pull applied to point C

G a pull applied to point A

H a push applied to point C

I a push applied to point B

43 The class is planning a trip to a local organic farm. According to this weather forecast, which days would be **best** for visiting the farm?

A Monday and Tuesday

B Tuesday and Wednesday

C Monday, Tuesday, and Wednesday

D Monday and Wednesday

44 Which of these describes a behavioral adaptation that helps the animal survive?

F Great gray owls hear the movement of mice and voles in meadows.

G Bats use echolocation to find insects in the night skies.

H A snowshoe hare's fur changes from brown to white.

I An Alaska brown bear hibernates through winter.

45 The Smith family is building a new house and wants to use renewable energy for electricity. Which energy source do they need?

A coal

B natural gas

C oil

D solar

46 Does this illustration show a solid, a liquid, or a gas, and how do you know?

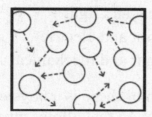

F It shows a liquid because it takes the shape of its container and the particles flow closely together.

G It shows a solid because the particles are close and compact.

H It shows a gas because the arrangement of particles is loose and the volume depends on the size of its container.

I It shows a solid because the particles appear in a regular, even pattern.

47 Which structure of this cactus provides protection from plant eaters?

A its large size

B its thick stems

C its deep roots

D its spines

48 What function do these leaves have?

F to get water from the soil

G to transport water through the plant

H to take in sunlight and carbon dioxide

I to produce flowers, fruit, and seeds

49 It is a nice summer day. Which reading on the thermometer **most likely** show the correct air temperature for this day?

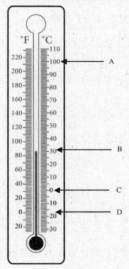

A A

B B

C C

D D

50 How does the state of ice change when it melts?

  F It changes from a solid to a liquid.

  G It changes from a gas to a liquid.

  H It changes from a solid to a gas.

  I It changes from a liquid to a gas.

51 You have a jar filled with types of uncooked macaroni. What would be the **best** way to sort the macaroni?

  A by color

  B by shape

  C by ingredients

  D by cost

52 Which of these resources can be replaced by humans?

  F a vein of gold in rock

  G a rushing river

  H a forest of trees

  I sand on a beach

53 A food web is shown below.

Which organism in this group is the top-level predator?

  A cricket

  B hawk

  C rabbit

  D toad

54 Which types of energy do we get from the sun?

  F chemical and heat

  G heat and light

  H light and electric

  I light and mechanical

55 Which of these is a physical adaptation that allows an animal to survive?

  A Japanese macaques soak in a hot spring to stay warm during winter.

  B Pufferfish can blow themselves up to twice their normal size to hold off predators.

  C Sandhill cranes migrate between Texas and the Arctic for breeding and food supplies.

  D Dolphins herd fish into bait balls to make it easier to catch their food.

56 Which method will allow you to separate two solids in a mixture?

  F using 100 mL water to separate salt from sugar

  G using a magnet to separate iron filings from sand

  H using a strainer to separate chocolate sauce from milk

  I using a magnet to separate iron and steel scrapings

57 Which space object is shown in the illustration?

A   asteroid

B   comet

C   meteor

D   moon

58 Which property of matter could be described as gritty, rough, or smooth?

F   luster

G   shape

H   smell

I   texture

59 A student questions how an object's height affects its potential energy. He designs an investigation and drops a golf ball from 0.5 m, 1 m, and 1.5 m into a bucket of flour, with the flour surface leveled. He predicts that the ball hitting the flour will make a crater and that the crater size will increase as the height from which the ball drops increases. What is the variable in this experiment?

A   the golf ball and the bucket of flour

B   the weight of each golf ball dropped

C   the height from which the ball drops

D   the size of the craters formed

60 Which of these is an example of a physical change caused by increased temperature?

F   an antacid tablet causing water to bubble

G   melting chocolate

H   frying an egg

I   an aluminum can being crushed

PLEASE NOTE

- Use only a no. 2 pencil.
- Example: ○ ● ○ ○
- Erase changes COMPLETELY.

FSSA Practice Test Form A

Mark one answer for each question.

1 Ⓐ Ⓑ Ⓒ Ⓓ	21 Ⓐ Ⓑ Ⓒ Ⓓ	41 Ⓐ Ⓑ Ⓒ Ⓓ
2 Ⓕ Ⓖ Ⓗ Ⓘ	22 Ⓕ Ⓖ Ⓗ Ⓘ	42 Ⓕ Ⓖ Ⓗ Ⓘ
3 Ⓐ Ⓑ Ⓒ Ⓓ	23 Ⓐ Ⓑ Ⓒ Ⓓ	43 Ⓐ Ⓑ Ⓒ Ⓓ
4 Ⓕ Ⓖ Ⓗ Ⓘ	24 Ⓕ Ⓖ Ⓗ Ⓘ	44 Ⓕ Ⓖ Ⓗ Ⓘ
5 Ⓐ Ⓑ Ⓒ Ⓓ	25 Ⓐ Ⓑ Ⓒ Ⓓ	45 Ⓐ Ⓑ Ⓒ Ⓓ
6 Ⓕ Ⓖ Ⓗ Ⓘ	26 Ⓕ Ⓖ Ⓗ Ⓘ	46 Ⓕ Ⓖ Ⓗ Ⓘ
7 Ⓐ Ⓑ Ⓒ Ⓓ	27 Ⓐ Ⓑ Ⓒ Ⓓ	47 Ⓐ Ⓑ Ⓒ Ⓓ
8 Ⓕ Ⓖ Ⓗ Ⓘ	28 Ⓕ Ⓖ Ⓗ Ⓘ	48 Ⓕ Ⓖ Ⓗ Ⓘ
9 Ⓐ Ⓑ Ⓒ Ⓓ	29 Ⓐ Ⓑ Ⓒ Ⓓ	49 Ⓐ Ⓑ Ⓒ Ⓓ
10 Ⓕ Ⓖ Ⓗ Ⓘ	30 Ⓕ Ⓖ Ⓗ Ⓘ	50 Ⓕ Ⓖ Ⓗ Ⓘ
11 Ⓐ Ⓑ Ⓒ Ⓓ	31 Ⓐ Ⓑ Ⓒ Ⓓ	51 Ⓐ Ⓑ Ⓒ Ⓓ
12 Ⓕ Ⓖ Ⓗ Ⓘ	32 Ⓕ Ⓖ Ⓗ Ⓘ	52 Ⓕ Ⓖ Ⓗ Ⓘ
13 Ⓐ Ⓑ Ⓒ Ⓓ	33 Ⓐ Ⓑ Ⓒ Ⓓ	53 Ⓐ Ⓑ Ⓒ Ⓓ
14 Ⓕ Ⓖ Ⓗ Ⓘ	34 Ⓕ Ⓖ Ⓗ Ⓘ	54 Ⓕ Ⓖ Ⓗ Ⓘ
15 Ⓐ Ⓑ Ⓒ Ⓓ	35 Ⓐ Ⓑ Ⓒ Ⓓ	55 Ⓐ Ⓑ Ⓒ Ⓓ
16 Ⓕ Ⓖ Ⓗ Ⓘ	36 Ⓕ Ⓖ Ⓗ Ⓘ	56 Ⓕ Ⓖ Ⓗ Ⓘ
17 Ⓐ Ⓑ Ⓒ Ⓓ	37 Ⓐ Ⓑ Ⓒ Ⓓ	57 Ⓐ Ⓑ Ⓒ Ⓓ
18 Ⓕ Ⓖ Ⓗ Ⓘ	38 Ⓕ Ⓖ Ⓗ Ⓘ	58 Ⓕ Ⓖ Ⓗ Ⓘ
19 Ⓐ Ⓑ Ⓒ Ⓓ	39 Ⓐ Ⓑ Ⓒ Ⓓ	59 Ⓐ Ⓑ Ⓒ Ⓓ
20 Ⓕ Ⓖ Ⓗ Ⓘ	40 Ⓕ Ⓖ Ⓗ Ⓘ	60 Ⓕ Ⓖ Ⓗ Ⓘ